REPORT
of an
INQUIRY
into an
INJUSTICE

CONTEMPORARY STUDIES ON THE NORTH

REPORT

of an

INQUIRY

into an

INJUSTICE

Begade Shutagot'ine and the Sahtu Treaty

PETER KULCHYSKI

UNIVERSITY OF MANITOBA PRESS

Report of an Inquiry into an Injustice:
Begade Shutagot'ine and the Sahtu Treaty
© Peter Kulchyski 2018

22 21 20 19 18   1 2 3 4 5

University of Manitoba Press
Winnipeg, Manitoba, Canada
Treaty 1 Territory
uofmpress.ca

Cataloguing data available from Library and Archives Canada
Contemporary Studies on the North, ISSN 1928–1722 ; 5
ISBN 978-0-88755-813-9 (PAPER)
ISBN 978-0-88755-545-9 (PDF)
ISBN 978-0-88755-543-5 (EPUB)

Cover design by David Drummond
Interior design by Jess Koroscil
Photographs by Peter Kulchyski
Map design by Weldon Hiebert, with information licensed under the
Open Government Licence – Canada

Printed in Canada

This book has been published with the help of a grant from the
Federation for the Humanities and Social Sciences, through the Awards
to Scholarly Publications Program, using funds provided by the
Social Sciences and Humanities Research Council of Canada.

The University of Manitoba Press acknowledges the financial support for
its publication program provided by the Government of Canada through
the Canada Book Fund, the Canada Council for the Arts, the Manitoba
Department of Sport, Culture, and Heritage, the Manitoba Arts Council,
and the Manitoba Book Publishing Tax Credit.

Funded by the Government of Canada | Canadä

CONTENTS

MAPS vi

OPENING BRIEF: *Concerning Begade Shutagot'ine Land Rights* 1

DEPOSITION ONE: *Tulita* 7

DEPOSITION TWO: *Caribou Flats* 60

DEPOSITION THREE: *Drum Lake* 93

DEPOSITION FOUR: *Stewart Lake* 137

CLOSING BRIEF: *Love Letter to Section 25 of the Canadian Constitution* 154

ACKNOWLEDGEMENTS 163

BIBLIOGRAPHY 165

PHOTOGRAPHS FOLLOW PAGE 86

A r c t i c

O c e a n

0 ___ 300
km

Deh Cho

●Colville Lake

●Fort
Good Hope

Norman●
Wells

●Deline

Tulita●   *Sahtu*

(Great Bear Lake)

YUKON

DENENDEH
(NORTHWEST TERRITORIES)

NUNAVUT

Yellowknife●

Fort Simpson●

River

Liard

Kakisa●

Tucho
(Great Slave Lake)

(*Mackenzie River*)

BRITISH COLUMBIA

ALBERTA

SASK.

MAN.

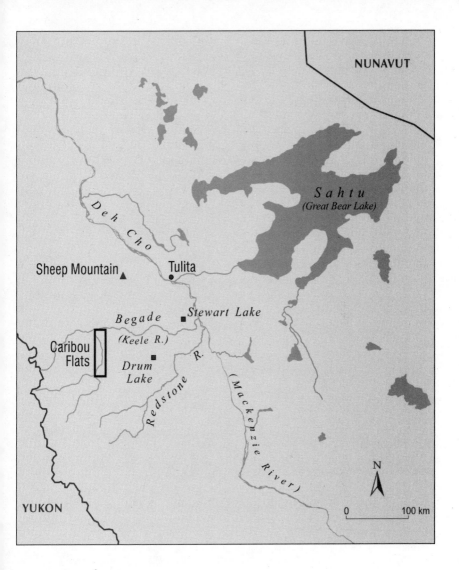

REPORT
of an
INQUIRY
into an
INJUSTICE

OPENING BRIEF
Concerning Begade Shutagot'ine Land Rights

I would like to tell the story of a people who tried to fight for their land. To do so, I will need to say a few things about the law of the land: Canada's law, Begade Shutagot'ine land.

In 1979 Justice Mahoney rendered a far-reaching legal decision that became a basis for how Aboriginal title is understood in Canadian law. The case was called *Hamlet of Baker Lake v. Minister of Indian Affairs and Northern Development*, and was a part of Inuit attempts to assert their Aboriginal title before mineral exploration in the region (particularly concerning uranium deposits that remain a site of contestation) rendered their title meaningless. The parts of Mahoney's decision that were adopted by higher courts and became enshrined in federal policy were his criteria for determining whether an Indigenous people had unsurrendered Aboriginal title. There were four such criteria:

1. That they and their ancestors were members of an organized society.
2. That the organized society occupied the specific territory over which they asserted Aboriginal title.
3. That the occupation was to the exclusion of other organized societies.

4. That the occupation was an established fact at the time sovereignty was asserted by England.

Catherine Bell and Michael Asch have patiently and painstakingly provided a strong critique of the case in Asch's collection of essays, *Aboriginal and Treaty Rights in Canada*, particularly the ethnocentrism of the first point, which came from Mahoney's reading of an earlier case of the Judicial Committee of the Privy Council of Great Britain called *Re Southern Rhodesia* (1919). Bell and Asch note that "all human beings live in society" (66) and reject the notion that societies can be placed on a hierarchy of development such that some are so low on an evolutionary scale that they cannot be seen to own their land. A second point of critical contention with the decision emerges from the third point, whether such occupation has to be to the "exclusion" of other groups in a cultural context where exclusive ownership of land was not relevant, and where sharing of lands and resources—aside from any concepts of ownership—was generalized.

Nevertheless, federal policy for the settlement of land claims in Canada continues to rest upon Mahoney's ethnocentric assumptions and uses almost his exact wording. The federal government adds three other criteria (I have added the numbers):

5. The aboriginal group can demonstrate some continuing current use and occupancy of the land for traditional purposes.
6. The group's aboriginal title and rights to resource use have not been dealt with by treaty.
7. Aboriginal title has not been eliminated by other lawful means. (Canada 2003)

Although I entirely agree with Bell and Asch and have made my own arguments about the necessity of revising the current assumptions behind modern treaty policy along with its substantive content, I want to sketch out the Begade Shutagot'ine claim for justice from within this unjust paradigm in order to demonstrate how strong their case actually is. That is, although the fact that a First Nation has to prove it was an "organized society," that it has to prove an occupation of land that "was to the exclusion of other organized societies," that such occupation "was an established fact at the time sovereignty was asserted by England," and that "aboriginal title was not eliminated by other lawful means" are to me all based on ethnocentric assumptions—even on the terrain of this lopsided playing field, Begade Shutagot'ine have a strong continuing claim to unsurrendered title over their traditional lands. What follows, then, is an opening brief as context to four depositions that I, Peter Kulchyski, inscribe as witness to Begade Shutagot'ine land rights struggles over the past two decades.

That they and their ancestors were members of an organized society: Begade Shutagot'ine existed and continue to exist as a distinct, widely recognized Dene Nation. They are acknowledged by the Dene Nation and by the Dehcho Tribal Council and treated as a distinct political and social group. Historical and anthropological records alike attest to their presence as a distinct group over a long period of time. The same records, which my work now joins, also attest to their "structure" or "organization" with, for example, a strong and elaborate structure of leadership.

That the organized society occupied the specific territory over which they assert aboriginal title: Again, the historical and anthropological records consistently show use and occupation of the Begade Shutagot'ine traditional territory to the west of the Deh Cho (Mackenzie River) along a seasonal cycle. Ancient legends tied to places, sacred places in themselves, the layers of stories and traces of villages and graveyards all clearly prove occupation of the area surrounding the river from which their name derives.

That the occupation was to the exclusion of other organized societies:
The Begade Shutagot'ine territory was traditionally very difficult
to reach; even with motorboats the shallow Begade (Keele River) is
nearly impossible to traverse upstream. In older times Begade Shutagot'ine families walked into the territory in fall and built a boat
to travel one way, downstream, along the Begade in spring/summer.
Other Dene peoples had their own territories; hence Begade use
and occupation of their traditional territory can be seen to be to
the exclusion of "other organized societies" in the early historic period. In more recent years the hunting lands up the Begade, especially
Caribou Flats, have been made more accessible by jet boat and bush
plane, and other Dene, as well as non-Indigenous hunters, have
come to make some use of the territory. But it is certain that the
territory *was* used and occupied primarily by Begade Shutagot'ine
until quite recently. Today as in the past there is little doubt that
Begade Shutagot'ine were willing to share their lands and resources, yet modern policies attempt to draw rigid lines where such lines
have no relevance. Begade Shutagot'ine occupied their land at least
as "exclusively" as did other contemporary successful Indigenous
land "claimant" groups, for example the Inuit of southern Kivilliq
regions, whose successful land claim includes territories also used by
Northlands and Sayisi Dene of northern Manitoba.

*That the occupation was an established fact at the time sovereignty
was asserted by England*: Occupation of this territory by Begade
Shutagot'ine reaches back into the time of myth, "when the world
was new," as the many stories about lawgivers, powerful helping
and malevolent beings, and historical ancestors attest to. Whether "England" can be said to have asserted its claim to sovereignty at
the time of the charter of the Hudson's Bay Company in 1610, the
Royal Proclamation of 1763, the travel up the Deh Cho in 1789, the

confederation of Canada in 1867, or the Rupertsland purchase in 1870, the Begade Shutagot'ine were on their lands.

The aboriginal group can demonstrate some continuing current use and occupancy of the land for traditional purposes: Begade Shutagot'ine still use and occupy their lands. This is evidenced by the many, many hunting trips I have engaged in with them, the stories of the many more they undertake in all seasons, their cabins, their snowmobile and jet boat and bush plane trips that still take them for longer or shorter stays onto their lands.

The group's aboriginal title and rights to resource use have not been dealt with by treaty: Both Treaty 11 and the Sahtu Treaty purport to "extinguish" Begade Shutagot'ine Aboriginal title. The many problems with Treaty 11, documented both in the court case *Re: Paulette*, by Justice Morrow, and in the book *As Long as This Land Shall Last*, by René Fumoleau, illustrate some of the problems with Treaty 11. The oral history of Paul Wright concerning his uncle Albert Wright's signature on the treaty offers a particular challenge to the validity of Treaty 11 as a tool of extinguishment of Begade Shutagot'ine lands. While the Sahtu Treaty likewise purports to extinguish Begade Shutagot'ine title, Begade Shutagot'ine attempts at the time to exclude themselves from that treaty, their petition to be excluded from it, and their boycott of the vote concerning it all very strongly call into question the validity of the Sahtu Treaty as a vehicle for extinguishment of Begade Shutagot'ine title. Begade Shutagot'ine have never explicitly agreed to surrender their title to their traditional lands. While some Begade Shutagot'ine individuals have, as individuals, signed on as beneficiaries of the Sahtu Treaty under pressure for the benefits or jobs they could access, their leaders have been courageous and steadfast in their refusal to do so.

Aboriginal title has not been eliminated by other lawful means: No "lawful means" of "eliminating" Aboriginal title can be achieved without the consent of the specific First Nation involved. This has been a founding legal fact in British North America and Canada since at least the Royal Proclamation of 1763. Begade Shutagot'ine have not given such consent.

Begade Shutagot'ine are a very small group of people numbering a few hundred. This, no doubt, is why government has found it easy to almost entirely ignore them. But the stakes of their struggle are very large indeed, involving as they do the continued surviving and thriving of a whole, distinct, unique people. Nothing in any decision of the Supreme Court of Canada or any constitutional document specifies that the size of a First Nation will be used in determining its Aboriginal rights. Nothing in the criteria for establishing a land claim, enumerated and discussed above, says that the size of the group is in any way a factor in making such a decision.

Begade Shutagot'ine are the continued owners of their land; they have unextinguished Aboriginal title to their traditional territories, an unrestricted right to enjoy their customs, practices, and traditions on those territories, and a fundamental right to be consulted and to be able to say "no" or negotiate appropriate compensation for any resource development projects that may take place on those territories. They are in position to negotiate a modern treaty that is acceptable to them if at some point they so desire. All of these statements—except, recently, the question of whether or not they can say "no"—are "facts of law" in Canada at this time: that they are not facts of life, that they continue to be blatantly ignored by federal and territorial authorities is therefore a violation of Canada's own claim to legitimacy and a profound injustice.

DEPOSITION ONE
Tulita

The very fact and essence of resistance is our humanity. We resist
dehumanization because we are human. And, I emphasize, our
resistance may not, need not, be beautiful, for dehumanization is not
a thing of beauty. Our expressions may most certainly be angry, even
"bitter," but that is for us to determine. As long as there remains
injustice, there will be anger.

—EMMA LAROCQUE

In indigenous cultures the core values of equality and respect
are reflected in the practices of consensus decision making and
dispute resolution through balanced consideration of all interests
and views. In indigenous societies, governance results from the
interaction of leadership and the autonomous power of the
individuals who make up the society. Governance in an indigenous
sense can be practiced only in a decentralized, small-scale
environment among people who share a culture. It centres on the
achievement of consensus and the creation of collective power.

—TAIAIAKE ALFRED

The primary experience of dispossession is what tends to fuel the
most common modes of Indigenous resistance to and criticism
of the colonial relationship itself: that is, Indigenous struggles

against capitalist imperialism are best understood as struggles
oriented around the question of land—struggles not only for land,
but also deeply informed by what the land as a mode of reciprocal
relationship (which is itself informed by place based practices
and associated forms of knowledge) ought to teach us about living
our lives in relation to one another and our surroundings
in a respectful, nondominating, and nonexploitative way.

—GLEN SEAN COULTHARD

The Dehcho Assembly, 1995

In the southwest portion of the Northwest Territories (Denendeh)
is a region called the Dehcho, at least by the Dene who have joined
a number of their communities together in a "Dehcho tribal council." Communities such as Fort Simpson, Hay River, Fort Resolution,
Jean Marie River, Trout Lake, Kakisa, and Fort Liard have used the
Dehcho Tribal Council to articulate their position on the issue of
a modern treaty/comprehensive land claim, and to express their demands regarding self-government. The Dene here are South Slave
Dene, at least so the anthropologists style them. The region led the
way in rejecting the 1989 global agreement in principle (AIP), a draft
comprehensive land claim that offered all Dene and Metis in the territory nearly half a billion dollars in exchange for the extinguishment
of their Aboriginal title. What most Dehcho Dene wanted instead
was a modern treaty that affirmed Aboriginal rights and reaffirmed
the principles or promises embodied in their oral history of Treaty 11.

When the AIP fell apart, other regions began negotiating regional land claims to replace it. First off the mark were the Gwich'in,
far to the north on the mighty Deh Cho (Mackenzie River, as we
newcomers call it), who were under pressure because of the fact that
nearby Inuvialuit (peoples) seemed to be prospering, having signed

a land claim in 1985. Within two short years Gwich'in negotiated a deal based on the AIP, with their portion of the funds allocated based largely on the number of members of their nation. Like dominoes falling, the next region to negotiate a separate deal was the Sahtu, immediately south of the Gwich'in and also on the Deh Cho, in the area including and to the west of Sahtu (or Great Bear Lake, as most maps would have it). The Tlicho (formerly Dogrib) to the south and east of the Sahtu began negotiating their own agreement, finally signed in 2004. Although these agreements were all hotly contested, in each case leaders were trying to do the best they could for their peoples, find a solution that fit their particular circumstances, see what they could do within the parameters of a largely unjust policy framework.

To the southwest of Tucho (Great Slave Lake), Akaitcho's people (the Chipewyan, or Treaty 8 people in the Northwest Territories) attempted to negotiate an agreement based on a fundamentally different model, involving the rights promised through Treaty 8. To the west of Akaitcho's people, southwest of the Dogrib and south of Sahtu, were the Dehcho.

The Dehcho had decided at that time not to extinguish their Aboriginal title. They wanted to negotiate a separate territory for themselves, modelled on what they saw happening in Nunavut. This was anathema to the NWT government, who in their self-interest saw further division of the rump of the territory as "unrealistic." The Dehcho Tribal Council passed a declaration that committed themselves to maintaining, rather than extinguishing, their Aboriginal title.

Once a year, delegations from each of the Dehcho communities met in an annual assembly in order to discuss their positions on evolving issues, to elect leaders, and to engage in some social and cultural exchanges. In 1995, as in many of the years before and after, the Dehcho Assembly was held in Kakisa. Kakisa is a lovely, small community in the centre of the region, reachable by road and equidistant from the main communities of the Dehcho. It is situated on a small lake that provides fish for the local residents, who are generous and hospitable hosts. Most visitors stay in a campground, a few billet with friends. There was no hotel in 1995. Tourists often blithely drive by the turnoff to Kakisa, on their way to Yellowknife or perhaps Fort Simpson; at most they may come a few miles off the main highway to look at Lady Evelyn Falls, a sight worth seeing, and then continue on their way. It is a shame that they miss out on spending time in the community, though, because in spite of its accessibility by road it has the feel of a very traditional Dene village, with people living the rhythm inspired by the land.

The 1995 Dehcho Assembly was where I first met Paul Wright. At that time, I was completing the research that would years later be articulated in *Like the Sound of a Drum*. Although by then I had many friends from Fort Simpson, Eric Menicoche, who had been a student of mine in the south, was still my closest contact. Early on in the course of the four-day assembly, he introduced me to a cousin of his named Clarence Campbell, from the more northerly community of Tulita. Clarence seemed a serious and kind young man who was articulate and well-educated. We spoke about him attending university, and about me helping him put together some proposals for his community. I didn't realize that he had come with a delegation from his community, because at that time Tulita was not a community in the Dehcho Tribal Council; we spoke on the fringes of the circle in which formal presentations, speeches, and resolutions were taking place.

The meetings were held in a partially enclosed area with rafter-style seating, a diesel generator providing power for amplification and an independent contractor supplying equipment and facilities for interpreters to translate the proceedings. The agenda included presentations from federal and territorial government officials, the language commissioner of the NWT spoke at some point, and there was also an open agenda and time for delegates to discuss and pass resolutions. Each community had sent a delegation whose size was fixed, based on the population of the community. People drifted in and out of the formal meeting, catching up with friends or conducting politics or business on the side, particularly as some long-winded speech was following its casual course or as some esoteric procedural debate was unfolding. Usually the delegations included the chiefs, key councillors, important elders; but sometimes also community members who were interested in the issues or who had been summarily drafted to fill the quotas, or who volunteered in order to get some time out of town, visit friends, or get shopping done in the bigger and cheaper supermarkets of nearby Hay River. The days were hot and dry and lent an indolent atmosphere to the whole affair, in spite of the intensity and importance of many of the discussions: long hours of perfunctory talk were punctuated by powerful moments of debate laced with ringing declarations of principle and inspiring insights.

Standing outside of the meeting, near where the smokers usually gathered for their regular breaks, holding on to the tea in the perennial Styrofoam cup that was my excuse for taking a break and leaving my seat, I suddenly sensed that something was happening. Everyone was moving quickly back into the meeting circle; the outside area had been deserted. Even the women who kept watch over coffee and tea, and many of the other hangers-on with no particular role at the meeting were hanging around the edges or seated inside the circle listening attentively. I scrambled back to my seat and fumbled with the headphones, since the speech was in Slavey. It was an elder talking, I could tell from the voice. He was talking about the treaty and the land claim, the need to work together. He didn't speak long, perhaps only ten or fifteen minutes, and I had missed much of it. But the electricity in the air, generated by the extraordinary power of his words reflected in the attentiveness of all the Dene there, let me know that this was somehow important. As he spoke I scanned the circle, trying to find the body behind the voice. It turned out that he was almost right in front of me. I could see a heavyset older man, the back of his head, red braces holding up his pants. He ended his speech by saying something about how he hoped everyone would leave with "good stories," would take these good stories back to their communities. When he was done, even though business continued, the room cleared as if it was time for a coffee break.

Later, outside the circle, I asked Eric who that was; he said with a somewhat surprised tone, as if I should already know, "That's Paul Wright!"

That afternoon, in the last session of the day, when Wright spoke again I was in my seat and knew enough not to leave. I watched as people alertly refilled the room. This time the main thrust of his speech was that his people needed help. He said he wanted help from the Dehcho Tribal Council. He wanted help from anyone who could assist them. He insisted that his people didn't want the Sahtu land claim, didn't want to give up their land. They needed help. He needed help. All this was in Slavey, which I understood through the interpreter. I saw something else: Clarence, whom I had already met and talked to several times, was at his side.

After the meeting I approached Clarence and asked if there was any way I could be of use. He said to come that evening and talk to Paul, that he would interpret, and that he was sure I could indeed be of help; in fact, his earlier talk with me about proposals had really been to solicit my assistance.

Many hours later, under long shadows cast by a sun that barely dipped below the horizon, sitting around a fire with people I would come to know well (though at that time all were strangers to me), forms lit by the flickering luminescence cast by the firelight—I was introduced to Paul Wright.

Instead of listening, just listening, I explained, my words tumbling out. I was a professor. I could help in various ways: writing proposals, holding workshops, helping make connections with people in the south. I worked for First Nations for free because the university paid me a good salary. It would be an honour to work with him. He had an aura of kindness and strength about him. He had already decided that I was a "good man." He thanked me. His "masi cho" sank deeper, seemed to come from some well of gratitude, than the commonplace expression had ever resonated for me. There was another elder with him, Gabe Etchinelle. Slowly, as the faces of the small group from Tulita came into focus, I began to sort out those who spoke English from those who didn't. Talk circulated in Slavey. Small bits would be translated for me. A few of my words would get translated back. My timing. Their timing. Who would be where, when? When would we intersect? Could plans be changed? Need they be changed? What must be done? Out of that late evening talk a plan for the days to come was formed. We would all meet up in Yellowknife. There, I could try to help them write a declaration for the Begade Shutagot'ine.

As far as I have been concerned to notice about myself and many of the people I know, life mostly runs its course and I only rarely drag myself outside of the numbing routines, endless repetitions, base boredom of existence. Even actual events when they actually happen—this degree is conferred, this partner leaves, this parent dies—seem to unfold so slowly, so predictably, that I don't live the moment, the experience. I wait and wait and when I'm done waiting, sure enough, an event has transpired, an event has taken place. I can look back on it, in fondness or anguish. Did I live it? Did it happen?

In the summer of 1995 at the Dehcho Assembly in Kakisa, something happened.

Begade Shutagot'ine

On old maps of the Deh Cho, there is a river to the south of the community labelled Fort Norman, now called Tulita. This river runs down from deep in the mountains far to the west of the Deh Cho. On these maps the river is called Gravel River, an apt, descriptive name. Later it would come to be called the Keele River, as it is today. In Slavey, gravel river is *begade*. The mountains this river flows through are today known as the Mackenzie Mountains. Again, in Slavey mountain is *shuhta*. Also in Slavey, the word for people is *Dene* or *t'ine*. Begade Shutagot'ine [bay-gah-day shoe-tah-goh-tin-nay], then, are the Gravel River Mountain People. There are other mountain Dene, other rivers that flow into the Deh Cho from the mountains, hence the need to specify which mountain Dene are being discussed.

You can learn something about the Begade Shutagot'ine from a National Film Board of Canada film made in the 1970s, called *The Last Moose-Skin Boat*. The film was made by a Dene from Tulita, Raymond Yakeleya. It documents a hunting camp in the mountains, the hunting of moose, the process involved in making a large moose-skin boat, including the labour of both women and men, and the travel of that boat down the Begade to Tulita. The narrator of the film is Gabe Etchinelle. The last moose-skin boat now sits in a special place of honour, as a prized exhibit, in the Prince of Wales Museum in Yellowknife.

The film tells us that Gravel River Mountain Dene, in the period of their early contact with newcomers, became specialists as meat provisioners. They hunted moose, caribou, and Dall sheep, bringing the meat down from the mountains in spring in moose-skin boats to provision the fur trade posts and provide meat for those Dene so absorbed with trapping furs that they needed help with subsistence. Later in the summer season, they would begin the long trek, on foot, back into the mountains: moose-skin boats were made to go one way, downriver.

Today most of the Begade Shutagot'ine live in the community of Tulita, on the junction of the Deh Cho and the Sahtu Deh (Great Bear River). Tulita is a small community, with a population of about 600. In older times, about half of these people were based at a lake to the east and inland of the Deh Cho: Willow Lake people. The other half are Begade Shutagot'ine.

The Etchinelles and the Andrews are the largest of the Begade families, but Campbells and Wrights also belong with them. They tend to live clustered toward the south end of town, closest to the mouth of the river that lies many kilometres further south and leads into their traditional territories. When they can afford it, they prefer to buy and use jet boats, which instead of relying on propellers that extend a foot or so deeper in the water than the keel of the boat, use a jet propulsion system that is set inside the bottom of the boat. Since the Begade is such a shallow river, people using this kind of boat can actually traverse the many sunken sandbars and with luck, with high waters, with knowledge of the river, with a degree of determination, and with a light-enough load actually make it to the fabled hunting grounds far to the west amidst the mountains. The jet boats, though, use a lot of gas.

Begade Shutagot'ine are proud of their history as food suppliers to their own Dene people and to the newcomers. They continue to be proud of their hunting abilities, especially their ability to hunt the very difficult mountain sheep, whose meat is prized.

One time I travelled by canoe down the famed Nahanni River, or Nahe Deh. My partner was inexperienced and I not up to the task, not able to properly compensate. We dumped and had a harrowing time returning to safety (though, really, I like to say I did canoe the Nahe Deh and just happened to go about 100 metres with the canoe upside down!). Eventually when we got to the small hamlet of Nahanni Butte, someone took pity on us and gave us some ground meat to cook. I remember savouring it, something I had never tasted. When I found out it was sheep meat I thought I would likely never taste it again. Little did I then know that a half-decade later I would have the great privilege of spending time with the best mountain sheep hunters in the world.

Tulita is the furthest south of the five communities in the Sahtu region. The Begade Shutagot'ine, living as they do in the southern part of Tulita, with traditional territory in the southernmost part of the Sahtu, abut the next Dene region to the south: the Dehcho. In the early 1990s the Sahtu Tribal Council negotiated a comprehensive land claim, or modern treaty. The agreement included a clause that extinguished their Aboriginal title to all of their traditional territories. This is something that the Begade Shutagot'ine whom I talked with were strongly opposed to. They did not want to surrender their traditional territories. But they also did not want to prevent the rest of the Sahtu communities from going ahead with a land claim, including that part of Tulita that supported it. They came up with a number of strategies: petitioning the minister of Indian Affairs; boycotting the vote on the claim; and, in order to secure allies and clearly show how distinctive they were, how they did not support while not opposing the Sahtu claim, joining the Dehcho Tribal Council. In the summer of 1995 a delegation of Begade Shutagot'ine travelled down to Kakisa for the Dehcho Assembly to tell their story.

In Ethel and Leon's Kitchen

Back in Yellowknife, a few days after the Dehcho Assembly, I called the number I had been given. The woman who answered was expecting my call. Yes, Paul was there. Yes, he remembered me and he still wanted to meet with me. This afternoon was fine. She gave instructions about how to find her house. Her name was Ethel.

Ethel Blondin-Andrew, for much of the '90s and into the new century, was the member of Parliament for the whole of the western Arctic, for what is now called the Northwest Territories and what I with many Dene friends prefer to call Denendeh. She was one of a very few Indigenous members of Parliament; she was appointed Secretary of State for Youth by Jean Chrétien. As a member of the federal cabinet, she acted as one of the senior elected Indigenous politicians in Canada. Although Ethel is part of the extended Blondin family that comes from Deline, the Andrew in her name that comes from her husband, Leon, connects her by marriage to Begade Shutagot'ine. Hence, in Ethel the Begade Shutagot'ine had a kind of privileged access to the corridors of power. She worked assiduously on their behalf.

It was only when I actually arrived at Ethel's house that I realized whom I was dealing with. By then we had already struck a casual tone, and we were meeting on northern ground, where formalities generally give way to relaxed hospitality. For many of the hours that followed Ethel acted as translator so that Paul, Gabe, and I could communicate. She clearly also played a role in her own right: added explanations and attempted to fill in gaps she thought were important, knowing how little I knew.

We sat down for tea in the kitchen. Paul and Gabe began to speak, talking about the Sahtu Treaty, the injustice being done to their people, talking about who their people were, the many rivers and mountains that they associate with their territory, with their sense of self. Ethel interpreted, adding explanations and a few stories about the two. It came out that they wanted me to draft some sort of a declaration for the Begade Shutagot'ine, in English. I said I would be honoured to try. Out of his nylon jacket pocket Paul pulled several sheets of paper. I could see across the table that they were covered in syllabic writing. He began to read. Ethel translated. I wrote.

It was difficult to follow, but two aspects of it were clear to me: there was some kind of explanation of who Begade Shutagot'ine are, of their distinctiveness from other Dene nations, of the rivers and mountains they are attached to; and there was an insistence that they did not want to surrender their Aboriginal title through a land claim, that they wanted to reaffirm the sharing relationship with newcomers they saw articulated or specified in Treaty 11. It was at least an hour before he was finished. We arranged that I would go home and work that night on a draft of a declaration based on what Paul had said—though Gabe had a few words to add, he in the end didn't get a chance to read from the piece of paper he had prepared—and meet again the next day to go over it with them and discuss our next move.

The enormity of what I was supposed to try was somewhat overwhelming. I was still only beginning to understand the situation of Begade Shutagot'ine. I wanted to stick close to Paul's words, as close as possible, but they had a logic of their own that I was unable to entirely follow. In those days I needed more structure to give something coherence. I felt that something close to poetry was demanded. I was also told that the whole statement had to be at most a page and a half, ideally a page, long. I had about ten pages of notes. I wrote something that tried to use poetic repetition to convey the style of repetition that Paul deployed, that tried to convey who the Begade Shutagot'ine were in terms of the many unfamiliar places that had been named for me, and that made the point about land claims and treaties and rights. In the end, as always with my first draft of something, I was quite pleased with the result.

The next day we gathered again in the kitchen at Ethel and Leon's house. While I was eager to read out the fruits of my labour, they were eager to talk more, explain more, add details to what they had told me yesterday but hadn't had time to flesh out. And, of course, there was tea to be made and drunk. Eventually I passed the two pages on to Ethel, letting her know this was only a draft but that I hoped it would make a good start. She read out loud, translating the text into Slavey. It became clear that it wouldn't do. No doubt too much of me in those words, not enough of what Paul was looking for. No one criticized directly or sharply, but there was a sense that it wasn't what they were asking for. Ethel at one point said, "I can see what you are trying to do, but . . ." and that was as far as it got. We turned to other things and I never again was asked to help draft a declaration. Such a document was never drafted. My friends from the Dehcho region, fresh from having published the Dehcho declaration, had been dubious about the idea from the start, perhaps feeling that too many new declarations would have the effect of mitigating the impact of their own, and something of this concern may have been conveyed to Paul. In any event, my own efforts were not successful. It appears, though, that something else both more ephemeral and more tangible had developed. By attempting to work on this, we had slowly come to know each other in a small way. I had come to appreciate how extraordinary these two men were and feel comfortable in their presence; not too intimidated to relate as friends, not too oblivious to respect their commitment, their principles, their knowledge, their very being. Paul had already decided that I had a "good heart," that we would try to work together.

Talk turned to logistics. When could I come to Tulita? Could I travel with them on their return journey? Places that had a mythic sound to me—Drum Lake, Caribou Flats, Bear Rock, Red Dog Mountain—these were held before me like a promise. I would have to see them, I was told. The names of these places became like talismans. To understand the Begade Shutagot'ine I would have to spend time with them, travel to their territory. Should I apply for research money? Would they give me a letter of support? There was much to discuss, but we got through enough for me to feel like a proper beginning was made. I would indeed travel back with them to Tulita, and eventually travel up the Begade, past Red Dog Mountain to Caribou Flats by jet boat, fly in a chartered plane to Drum

Lake, dance to the sound of Dene drums at the foot of Bear Rock in Tulita, and learn a little bit about Begade Shutagot'ine ways.

At that time I was perhaps a bit star-struck. I remember savouring the moments, thinking, "How often will I be talking politics with two respected elders in a member of Parliament's house, with her acting largely as translator?" This was one of those few times when the moment itself, strong as it was, was not as important as the moments that would result.

Paul Wright

Paul was a large man, with what is called salt-and-pepper hair, which was also the shade of the stubble often on his chin. He had a deep, rolling laugh, "heh heh heh," and he used it often. He carried himself with a great, innate sense of humility and dignity. But it was also as if a spirit of delight danced in the twinkles in his eyes.

When he prayed, he would touch his heart; when he listened to the prayers of others, he folded his arms across his chest and buried his hands in his armpits, bowing his head. He was a lay preacher, and when no one else was available he would conduct Sunday services out at his camp or in town.

Paul was a nephew of Albert Wright, a former chief whose name can be found on Treaty 11. He had seen millennia's worth of change in his lifetime: from hearing Dene creation stories as a child or bursting with pride at having earned his first high-powered rifle, to travelling by jet boat with his ever-present video camera or visiting Ethel Blondin-Andrew in Ottawa and meeting the prime minister. For much of his adult life he was chief of the small community then called Fort Norman, now Tulita.

He had the ability to make people feel good about themselves and to help them find the best part of themselves. As a political leader, at least while I knew him, he never spoke against anyone, even though there were strong feelings and very different positions being taken, even within his home community. His was a politics of trying to do the best, trying to be the best; he never needed an enemy to call down in order to build himself up, because he never needed to build himself up.

He had a kind of compassion for people, for anyone. One time, he told me, he had been to Ottawa. He was walking near his hotel and spotted a young woman trying to get food from a garbage can. It bothered him deeply. He wondered if she wouldn't be better off coming back to Tulita with him, but had no way of talking to her. In the end there was nothing to do but pass her by without being able to offer any help, and that bothered him too. He felt bad for the poor people in Ottawa; they had no way of hunting meat if they were hungry.

His time as chief involved great events: the forging of the Dene Nation, the struggle against the pipeline, the struggle for control of the government of the Northwest Territories, the initiation of land claim negotiations, the achievement of Aboriginal rights in the Constitution. Many times, when the leadership of the Dene Nation needed to meet in a place where they could, in peaceful, serene surroundings, talk enough to work out a position, they would come to Paul's camp in the Mackenzie Mountains: Drum Lake.

The story I heard, perhaps from Ethel, may not be true but it seems to fit. Paul's marriage partner was named Mary Rose. They were not able to have children, so they adopted. In spite of many changes and even more difficulties, they lived a good life, spending as much time as they could in their beloved mountains; no doubt spending too much time apart as Paul travelled to meetings and carried the many obligations of a chief. In the world being shaped around us, couples who hate each other are often cast together in an enforced bondage that resembles a Sartrean *No Exit*, while couples deeply in love struggle to be able to spend any time together. Mary Rose and Paul were a loving couple, by all accounts. When she died ahead of him he grieved deeply. He went back into the mountains, to Drum Lake, and mourned and healed as best as he could.

Meanwhile, around him the world continued to turn. Politics was politics. Around the time of Mary Rose's death, a major Dene land claims agreement fell apart, much to Paul's relief, since it contained a clause surrendering Aboriginal title to Dene lands. When he returned from the bush two years later, his own community and region were in the process of settling a claim based on those same premises. He started to ask questions: "Why are we doing this?" "Is it right?" "Isn't this what we said we'd never do?" and was not satisfied with the answers he got. Slowly, inexorably, he was drawn back into the world of politics and spent the last years of his life there.

One time, Paul came with David Etchinelle to Trent University to visit me, as part of a Northern Chair lecture series I had helped to organize—with my friends Bella and Frank T'seleie—called *Dene ke* (Dene Ways). They were impressed with my ability to negotiate the backstreets of Peterborough in my little car, saying I knew the roads like they knew their river. At a small meeting held on the Symons campus, a publicity photographer and a writer from the university came to take a photo for the university's newsletter. They asked if they could photograph Paul while he sang in prayer, and he said "fine, fine," smiling broadly. When he was done his prayer they came up to me, deeply moved, asked me to thank him, thanked me for inviting and hosting him, and continued to linger, hoping perhaps that some small part of his presence might ignite a flickering spark in their spirits. Such was his impact on people. Later, one of those photos would appear in a corner of the poster produced for the university's fundraising campaign.

When he restarted his political career, Paul was among the oldest of the Begade Shutagot'ine. But there was another, older than he: Gabe Etchinelle. Gabe was also living on his own and the two, separated by ten years, began to travel and work together. They became a kind of odd couple, Gabe tall and lean, Paul on the portly side (Gabe once, in a teasing aside to me, said, "Big fat Paul"!), the two trying to make sense of the letters and pamphlets and agreements they got from the government or their own elected leaders, the two trying to change the mysterious currents of history that were taking their lands away from them, the two trading stories from harder but simpler times, the two giving each other some comfort and understanding beyond speech, teasing each other or commiserating: friends.

Somehow, I never learned how, Paul acquired a video camera. He would make videos of his travels. These would often feature the planes taking off, or some of the many hours he spent in meetings and assemblies, or the daily rhythm of life in other communities. When I visited he would ask: "Do you want some stories?" I, researcher-excited, would answer an eager "yes," anticipating some mythical or historical lesson, and then try not to show my disappointment as the television was turned on and I got the chance to watch yet another plane landing, another crowd of people getting off and meeting their relatives. . . . Later, I would hear the kinds of stories I wanted to hear. But Paul loved his video camera, loved to make those little stories of his travels and loved to show them. The very least any of us could do was watch.

Paul spoke some English; his Dene was powerfully expressive and some of that power carried over into his English. Gabe spoke very little English; perhaps he understood a bit more. One time, Paul said to me, "The problem is, everyone is speaking all these different languages. We should get everyone to speak just one language, that way everyone could talk to each other and we wouldn't have these difficulties, these problems."

"Yes, but what language should everyone in the world speak?"

The answer was obvious: "Dene!"

There are a very few people we may be lucky enough to meet who remind us of what it is possible for human beings to be at their best; who draw our highest out of ourselves; who in their very being make us believe in possibility hope goodness; who so clearly give so much of themselves that this giving must come from the deepest part of some valley of pain where a border is crossed, leaving only a kind of compassion for all the others mired in some part of that darkness; whose hard-won wisdom is the wisdom of kindness; whose hard-won strength is the strength of kindness; whose eyes whose words whose touch are the sight sound feel of kindness. Such was my fortune that I was able to meet and work with a man of this character: Paul Wright.

Again, again, as with the Begade Shutagot'ine declaration, I write Paul with my words, the wrong words, but the only ones I have. And now there is no Paul to gently correct me, so I must live with what I inscribe, and will never do my subject justice and must, still, try.

This much, though, can be written with assurance: Paul Wright was Begade Shutagot'ine.

The Sahtu Treaty

The Sahtu region is made up of five communities: Fort Good Hope, Norman Wells, and Tulita on the Deh Cho, Deline on Sahtu, and Colville Lake on the lake that bears its name. Fort Good Hope and Deline are the larger Dene and Metis communities in the region and tend to carry the most weight. Norman Wells is an oil town, the head of a pipeline that carries oil all the way down to Zama, Alberta, and hence includes a large non-Indigenous presence as well as Dene from the other communities and a somewhat larger Metis presence. It is the largest community in the region and has the most services available, but also has a frontier resource town character rather than the feel of Dene or Metis communities. Tulita and Colville Lake are the smallest communities in the region, though Colville is significantly smaller even than Tulita.

There is a way in which Sahtu comprises a kind of inverted symmetry: Colville Lake, on a small lake inland, is related and connected to the larger Fort Good Hope on the Deh Cho. Further south, Tulita on the Deh Cho is related and connected to the larger Deline, which is on a large lake inland.

In 1994 the final agreement between the government of Canada and the Sahtu Dene and Metis was signed. The Sahtu Treaty is one of the few comprehensive land claims or modern treaties to have been signed with First Nations who are already treaty signatories, in this instance Treaty 11 (1921). The reserves promised in Treaty 11 were never set up, and there were enough other irregularities associated with it that after some struggle, Dene and Metis in Denendeh were able to restart treaty negotiations in the 1970s. A global Dene and Metis agreement for the territory, finally prepared in 1989, fell apart when the Dehcho and Akaitcho communities insisted that Aboriginal title not be surrendered. Their insistence was inspired in part by the then recent Supreme Court of Canada decisions, announced in January of that year, regarding Sparrow and Sioui. In the Sparrow case, from BC, the Aboriginal rights promised in section 35 of the Constitution were characterized as meaningful rights (not an "empty box") that had a significant role in conflicts over resource use. In the Sioui case, from Quebec, released at nearly the same time, treaties were cast as documents where "the honour of the Crown" was at stake, and therefore a "liberal and generous" interpretation was demanded.

Together these cases implied a significant ratcheting up of the value of Aboriginal and treaty rights, so the hesitation to extinguish those rights in the immediate wake of the two decisions made sense, in spite of the fact that a $450 million agreement was being threatened. When Dene and Metis asked that the agreement in principle be reopened to new negotiations based on the new legal reality, the federal government took a hard line and refused. The federal government then moved quickly to negotiate with those Dene willing to sign deals on a regional basis. First the Gwich'in, in 1991, negotiated a treaty based on the 1989 agreement. Then, in 1994, the Sahtu settled a land claim, called the Sahtu Treaty, also modelled largely on the 1989 deal, though with some differences.

In the Sahtu Treaty, Sahtu Dene and Metis agreed to "cede, release, surrender and convey all rights, titles and interests, if any, to all lands and waters in Canada to her majesty in right of Canada forever." These are the words of the extinguishment clause, the preferred mechanism for achieving certainty of land title, the federal government's stated goal in negotiating comprehensive land claims. In exchange for surrendering what were often characterized as "undefined title and rights," Dene and Metis received the benefits articulated in the claim ("defined rights"). These included a $75 million cash settlement, to be paid over a lengthy, multi-decade period; the establishment of land-use planning and a variety of other joint management boards; a promise to negotiate self-government agreements at the request of the Indigenous signatories; a small proportion of the taxation revenues that might be generated from resource development in the region; and two forms of land ownership, one including subsurface rights and one exclusively involving surface rights, to about 10 percent of the traditional Dene and Metis territories in the Sahtu.

There was much controversy, discussion, and debate about the Sahtu Treaty when an agreement in principle was brought back to the communities. I documented some of this from the perspective of Fort Good Hope and Fort Simpson in *Like the Sound of a Drum*. Communities like Colville Lake and Tulita wanted to be able to "opt out" of the land claim; they wanted the final vote to be tabulated on a community-by-community basis. Those communities that accepted the deal could go ahead, those that rejected it could be removed. These parameters, this degree of flexibility, was denied them. It would be an all-or-nothing acceptance or rejection for the whole region. In the short space of about eight months, people were told to cast their votes on a deal that would determine their future and the future of the generations who would follow. The negotiators of the agreement went from community to community for information sessions that explained the agreement. No one who opposed the deal was given any funding to produce pamphlets or conduct workshops or support their position, so the "information sessions" were basically attempts to sell the deal. What debate took place occurred with one side holding all the resources it needed while the other side relied entirely on word of mouth and personally offered time. The agreement was ultimately endorsed by a healthy majority, and no community-by-community results were made available. It would be interesting to know how Colville Lake voted, for example. In Tulita, about one half of the community formally boycotted the vote: Begade Shutagot'ine.

The Sahtu Treaty also included clauses determining who was eligible to receive the benefits it promised. Eligible Dene and Metis were called "beneficiaries" and had to sign up by a certain date. This gave them the right to vote on the agreement and the right to share in its benefits, including financial "payouts." Many Begade Shutagot'ine, as well as boycotting the vote for the agreement, also refused to sign up as beneficiaries.

After the settlement of the Sahtu Treaty, new boards and bodies were created. Political leaders moved from being land claim negotiators to being corporate managers: they had to sit on the joint management boards that had been created, they had to set up and staff corporations at the regional and community-by-community level. At the everyday level, people immediately started to ask where the money was. Seventy-five million dollars sounded like a great deal of money. Where was it? To mute the dissent, the leaders in some communities started making cash payouts to beneficiaries of the agreement. To my mind, this was the worst possible use of the financial resources provided by the claim: instead of building up some form of financial heritage trust, money was being spent on satellite dishes and consumer products that would last a few years and disappear. This to satisfy the people who had been promised, or felt they had been promised, an immediate "better future" if they supported the claim. Instead, they received a few cash payments, some nice Christmas celebrations sprinkled with some big-ticket consumer items while the legacy of selling their lands slipped through their fingers. But there were leaders in the Sahtu concerned about this as well, diligently trying to be faithful stewards of the people's resources, trying to make the treaty work.

Then, as well, there were those who had boycotted the vote and who on principle refused to sign on as beneficiaries of the Sahtu Treaty in spite of clearly being entitled. Paul Wright and Gabe Etchinelle were among them. So were many other Begade Shutagot'ine, in spite of the fact that they had families, children whose legacy was also tied to the deal. They didn't get any cash payouts. Some were denied jobs among the many new positions being created, in spite of their qualifications, because they were "troublemakers." Some were offered cash payments retroactively if they would just "sign on." In small communities, the feelings generated by such exclusions and inclusions are white hot in their intensity. Gabe and Paul were deeply disturbed by what they saw going on around them, by what was happening to their people. The Sahtu Treaty made them "angry old men." Theirs was not the burning flash of uncontrollable rage found in the young; theirs was the slow, deep, thoughtful anger that led them to look steadily and directly into the eyes of anyone who defended the deal. There were not very many, if any, who could return their gaze.

The Secretary

One time, while I was taking notes in David and Theresa Etchinelle's house for some letter or other we would eventually send to some minister or other who would no doubt entirely ignore it by sending an empty polite reply, Paul turned to David and said, "We've sure got a good secretary," meaning me! As often as not, this was my role. I became Paul's secretary, and was proud to be placed in that role. At about the same time, in my southern role as department head and professor, my administrative assistant—the magnificent Joyce Miller—had confessed to me at a lunch meeting upon my question about what I could do to help her in her work, that she despised the "s" word she'd had to live with for so much of her life. I, quite clued out, asked, "What do you mean by the 's' word?" She, stunned a bit by my ignorance, replied, "Secretary!" So I worked diligently and successfully in that time of more humane bureaucracy to have her reclassified and paid as an "academic programs co-ordinator." While this was happening, I had myself achieved the status of "secretary" to Paul Wright, to Begade Shutagot'ine.

What, after all, could my role be? Although my oldest brother in his prime was an outstanding shot with a rifle and so a good hunter, I am a middling-to-poor shot, not a very good fisherman, not very useful at any of the many tasks required by bush life. My main attributes in camp are my willingness to put up with a lot without complaining, my generally good sense of humour, and my willingness to work hard at whatever menial tasks that an unskilled person of my ilk can contribute to. My contributions to Begade Shutagot'ine were that of scribe. I would write at their behest: letters, reports, proposals, applications, minutes, resolutions. As Paul said during that same session in Theresa and David Etchinelle's house, with me the "words would flow like a river." He liked the "sweet sound" of the way I would always try to express his thoughts, the unfailing politenesses I knew he wanted me to insert in the correspondence.

As well, of course, there is this, these words, which trace themselves across the blank whiteness of the virtual page here and now, in Kolkata, India, or Greifswald, Germany, or Winnipeg, Canada (and here and now, wherever some precious few of you find the space and time to read them), a lifetime away from the Deh Cho, two lifetimes away from Begade Shutagot'ine. What do these words amount to? Witness, I thought then, and still at times think that now. The witness function has become a critical category in social theory. The witness to historical trauma fashions a part of the historical record. Witness borrows a courtroom metaphor, overlaid in some uneasy fashion for us inheritors of a Christian legacy with a biblical metaphor: we bear witness, we testify, we hope our honest testimony will produce one small brick in that castle of justice we will never be able to enter.

My eyes, my ears saw and heard these men, who came from another era to live in our own and who spoke with deep feeling of justice. For them, justice was clear, nearly tangible: they knew it acutely and knew just as acutely when it had been violated. Perhaps this story repeats itself with every generation, but in this world with its peculiar dynamic of generational change, each generation has become a singularity. Among my generation, there were very few people such as Paul and Gabe. By witnessing their final years, I suppose in some ways I bear an afterimage of their singularity. I am one who tells the story they wanted me to tell and in my own body carry traces of it.

Historical trauma: these often-repeated words sit more lightly than they should, representing as they do an intergenerational wound resulting from a deeply painful singular event or series of events. An event, call it the conquest, still unfolds in many parts of the Americas. In each instance, for every single body that is folded beneath its logic, there is a pain that will be passed on to other bodies and will structure relations between people. Thinkers the calibre of Fredric Jameson (1988) refer to this as the history that hurts. Thinkers the calibre of Dominick LaCapra have carefully tried to understand what leads these histories to repeat themselves, compulsively, what role the historian has in working through such problems. Thinkers the calibre of Jean-Paul Sartre have called this hurt, this pain, this wound, this scar, an original violence. Thinkers the calibre of Jacques Derrida have called our attention to the "violence of the letter" (1992a) in that the scars may take the form of a trace, in that such wounds may not come from the blood of military conflict; such wounds may as easily be inscribed in anonymous office towers, traced onto digital storage devices, copied and faxed and posted to the World Wide Web. And so lives get changed, sometimes short-changed. It is bodies, what a thinker the calibre of Unamuno once called "[wo/]men of flesh and blood," that in daily miseries that need not exclude the worst kinds of violence turned inwards on the nearest bodies, miseries that also include the monotonies of despair, the spirit-killing boredom of lives without meaning, hope, purpose; it is bodies that exist this pain: historical trauma.

The witness is not the historian. The witness is sometimes a participant in the events she describes. The witness may also be, and is often thought of as, a bystander, a disinterested observer who happens to see some element or aspect of the event. In this instance, the historical trauma was the purported extinguishment of Aboriginal title of Begade Shutagot'ine through the mechanism of the Sahtu Treaty. Such extinguishment forms a link in the continuing process of dispossessing Indigenous peoples of the Americas to which historians give the name "the conquest." As witness, I was not an innocent bystander. I deliberately responded to the call of Begade Shutagot'ine for help, placed myself at their service, and now write these words. In these ways I became a participant in the events, and in a certain way attempted to advocate for Begade Shutagot'ine. But advocates have a different place than witnesses do in the courtroom drama. Can one be both? Not in a court of law, of course, but on that other stage, the stage of history, perhaps the boundaries are less rigid, more porous.

Do I have the right to do this, to write this? This is a story of the Begade Shutagot'ine, not my story. Why am I in it? What is my place? I find in writing it I cannot, much as I desire to, erase myself. These are not and cannot be Paul's words, except those few I indicate as his. These are my words, for better or worse. And the story of the story, of how I came to this story and came to be a small part of it, must be a part of its telling. I would like to tell the story of a people who tried to fight for their land. If I do not tell this story in writing, who will?

When I worked with Paul, I gained some stature among the Dene of Denendeh. I had earned some respect through my work with Fort Simpson and Fort Good Hope, and many knew me through my writings in *The Native Press* on Indigenous history (I wrote for a few years a biweekly column, which later became the basis of a book for Arbeiter Ring Press called *The Red Indians*); still, when I told people I was working with Paul Wright there was some intangible bit of feeling, some unstated acknowledgement, that this was a good thing for me to do, that it fit somehow, that I should be accorded a more weighty place among the political actors, researchers, politicians, policy analysts, journalists, community activists in Denendeh than I had previously been granted. This too was a measure of his light: it echoed off those who stood beside him. I too was a moon lit in the reflected glory of the rays that he projected. Alright, perhaps it wasn't quite so high-falutin'; I certainly was a better person under his influence.

Advocate, witness, scribe, secretary: perhaps the first three are my attempt to glorify the latter. Perhaps, like Joyce Miller, I find something demeaning in the "s" word. No doubt I did and do things that flow through all of these roles. But if it comes down to choices it won't come down to, I can indeed say that for a few years of my life I was filled to the brim with pride because I worked as Paul Wright's secretary.

Gabe Etchinelle

There was another elder who travelled with Paul, as I noted earlier. His name was Gabe Etchinelle. Many of the Begade Shutagot'ine, not only those in the extended Etchinelle family, called him "Uncle Gabe" or "Granpa." He was tall and thin and tough, his body forged and moulded by long walks in the mountains, carrying gear, carrying meat. He spoke relatively little English, though he was quite capable of dropping the odd wry, teasing comment ("big fat Paul") and appeared to understand somewhat more than he would speak. His bush knowledge was widely respected by Begade Shutagot'ine.

One time, in those empty moments, empty hours, as we waited for a plane to pick us up in the Mackenzie Mountains, having gorged ourselves on blueberries, Gabe showed Leon Andrew something, then Leon showed me. It was a tree that had gone unnoticed by the rest of us. On one side, the tree had been gouged by thick scratch marks. Leading up to that spot on the tree were indentations in the ground that had been created by years of repetition. "This is the tree," Leon told me that Gabe had said to him, "where the bear comes to get its power before it goes for its winter sleep." Leon then mimicked how the bear would walk and come to stand in front of the tree, filling the indentations in the ground with his own hands and feet, standing as a bear would stand, imitating the scratching. For Gabe the land was a book that long years of apprenticing had taught him to read; he found all kinds of mysteries and treasures that the rest of us casually overlooked, and, as often as not, he generously shared them.

Gabe is featured in the old National Film Board of Canada–sponsored film *The Last Moose-Skin Boat*. As the construction of the boat is finished, Gabe as narrator informs us that in the past the wise leaders of Begade Shutagot'ine would steer the boat down the river; now it was his turn. His tone is a mixture of being daunted by the task, worried about whether he would be up to it, and proud of being entrusted with the responsibility.

I too follow in some large footsteps. Norman Simmons, a wildlife biologist, helped establish the much-needed practice of working with an elder's knowledge when it came to assessing large mammal populations in his work with Gabe on Dall sheep in the Mackenzie Mountains. This approach would come to underwrite notions of joint management of lands and animal resources, theorized by my colleague Fikret Berkes at the University of Manitoba in his *Sacred Ecology*. Norman and Hilah lived and travelled with Begade Shutagot'ine for many more years than I have, and rendered many more services, becoming somewhat part of the extended Etchinelle family. I met them through one of Hilah and Norman's daughters, Deborah, now one of my closest friends, whom I encountered as a graduate student junior to me at York University in Toronto. Friends insisted we meet because we both seemed attached to the Northwest Territories. As a child she had participated in the camp where the moose-skin boat was made. Deborah's brother David also became a close friend and fellow reprobate, the kind of confidant a reprobate like me sorely needs. For the Simmons family, "Uncle Gabe" was the embodiment of goodness, wisdom, and kindness, and occupied the position in their hearts that Paul came to have in mine.

I had less contact with Gabe than with Paul, because I needed an interpreter and had to cross the boundary of language. Whenever I did get a small piece of time with him I exulted in it, though, and usually came away with some piece of information or insight that stayed with me. Such moments were rare such moments were precious such moments turned time into a treasure that cheated the measured linear steps we insist on calculating as if counting equals truth. In order to keep those moments I carefully placed them in the old trunk of stories that I could open and share at will: perhaps the best way I can say something about Gabe is to tell a few of these stories.

One time Gabe was in the hospital in Yellowknife. He was in his eighties when I met him, generally in good enough health that, unlike Paul, he made a strong contribution to camp life as butcher, as hunter. But he was also plagued with bouts of illness. Paul went to visit him in the Yellowknife hospital and I came along. For the most part they were silent on this visit, Paul sitting quietly beside the bed, Gabe sitting up in some discomfort on the bed. When an attending nurse left the room, though, Paul began to tease Gabe about finding a wife here and the two chuckled. It was a running gag with them— whenever they were in the presence of young women they wouldn't pass up an opportunity to get the first teasing word in about finding a wife. Eventually, not able to resist, I joined in this banter and would use whatever opportunities I found for similar teasing. Was the idea so far-fetched that it was truly harmless, as I then thought?

One time we had hunted several caribou. As they were being butchered Gabe had started a fire and begun to cook a batch of fresh ribs. Fresh-cooked caribou ribs, hung over an open fire, are a paradise for the palette. Gabe occasionally checked to see if the ribs were cooked. A pot of tea also bubbled merrily on the edge of the same fire. At some point, the ribs were ready, and he cut off the first piece and walked it over to hand it to me, sitting on a rock nearby. I was a bit stunned at the time at being so honoured. Perhaps it was a small way for him to say thank you to me: our trip was funded out of the research money I had secured for my work with the Begade Shutagot'ine. One of the small good things that I was able to contribute was to give Paul his last trip to Drum Lake, and Gabe his last trip to Caribou Flats. They gave me much in return, but I still think of that moment, that casual everyday gesture, as somehow particularly special, without really knowing why.

One time while we were camped at Caribou Flats in the Mackenzie Mountains, hunting moose caribou sheep, the camp had emptied out as we went off in boats to spend a day climbing and hunting the prized Dall sheep. Gabe and a few others were left to their own devices in camp. He had his rifle, since this was grizzly bear country and grizzlies could pose a serious danger, especially to a camp laden with meat and other food. We returned from a successful hunt, myself at least flush with the thrill of my first real mountain hunt. Gabe was sitting placidly, said a few words to James Etchinelle, one of the young men with us. Suddenly everyone was looking across the river, wanting to borrow my binoculars, looking through the telescope they also used. Then James got back into the boat. It seemed that a bull caribou had turned up across the Begade. Gabe brought it down from all the way across the river with one shot. It was the largest caribou we procured on that trip. Though Gabe was certainly old, he was rarely frail. Woe betide the caribou that thought it might catch him napping—though it is just as likely that Caribou had once again gifted itself to this old friend. Perhaps in his being he also posed a lightning-like danger to the bureaucrats who rule our time.

Gabe Etchinelle was Begade Shutagot'ine.

Treaty 11

To understand the position Begade Shutagot'ine took with respect to the Sahtu Treaty, one must understand something of their complex position on Treaty 11. Treaty 11 has its own history: last of the great numbered treaties of the Canadian north and west, it was negotiated in 1921 and 1922. As with other treaties, the main impetus came from demands on Indigenous lands being made by the newcomers. The treaties on the prairies had been sparked by a need for agricultural land for the waves of settlers who would come to repopulate this territory and whose number would eventually include my own forebears: these were the first seven of the numbered treaties, negotiated in the period 1871 to 1877 by Alexander Morris and documented in his great book *The Treaties with the Indians of Canada.* Treaties 8 to 11 pertained to more northerly regions; Treaty 8 included a part of Denendeh south of Great Slave Lake. These treaties were inspired by the "discovery" of some valuable natural resource, such as gold in the Yukon for Treaty 8. Unlike the earlier treaties negotiated by Morris, who as an official with some stature was empowered to make concessions, as he did in the case of Treaty 3 and Treaty 6, each northern treaty was conducted by a different team of lower-level officials whose job was simply to get the signatures onto the pre-established treaty document. These officials had no scope for vision or ability to even comprehend the broader significance of the task they were engaged in (the presence of poet/official Duncan Campbell Scott in the Treaty 9 official government delegation notwithstanding).

In the case of Treaty 11, although Dehcho Dene had been advocating for a treaty to help alleviate economic distress, it was Dene knowledge regarding oil at present-day Norman Wells that led government to have an interest in the region, and therefore a willingness to incur the expense of trying to extinguish Aboriginal title. A treaty was prepared in Ottawa, using much the same wording that had been used in the previous ten numbered treaties. A treaty party consisting of an Indian agent, a clerk, a few RCMP officers, a bishop, and mostly Metis interpreters began the arduous journey up the Deh Cho, stopping at each major camp where the year before it had been announced that treaty meetings would take place.

Compared to earlier treaties, the historical lateness of Treaty 11 (1921) meant it was possible for researchers in the late 1960s and early '70s to compile direct oral history from some of the remaining Indigenous participants in treaty negotiations. In fact, in the early '90s I met a Metis elder in Fort Good Hope whose older brother had been a treaty interpreter in Fort Resolution and who himself as a young teen had been present for the meetings. The work of both Morrow's court, discussed below, and of the priest/poet/historian/photographer

René Fumoleau could in part be based on direct witness testimony, while other treaties, where a strong oral history does exist, still involved indirect ("as told to"; "as told by") forms of testimony.

No doubt the Treaty 11 negotiators were in something of a hurry, moving downriver on the Deh Cho, with many places to visit and a desire to complete the work and return upriver before freeze-up, which comes earlier in the north. The lengthy speeches of Dene leaders, who did see the historical importance of the moment, were perhaps a bit tedious to some of these gentlemen. Their job, as they saw it, was to get signatures on a document. Most northern Dene in the '20s did not have European literacy skills; they had their own orders of literacy that did not translate well on paper documents. Most of the Dene signatures on Treaty 11 are X-style crosses. One can't help, when one looks at these, but be struck by the fact that so many of the X's are so similar. On earlier treaties the signatures are varied in form, sometimes with clan symbol markers, sometimes with an X where the lines barely or do not cross each other: "The white man wants us to mark the paper, we'll do so," these lines seem to say. Where so many X's are so similar, it is likely they were put there by the clerk, with the Dene "signatory" perhaps touching the pen to signify assent. Perhaps.

The possibility of fraud in such a circumstance, signing on someone's behalf, becomes very real. Who would ever find out? Who would know? There are other irregularities with respect to Treaty 11. The story of the replacement of an unfavourable chief in Fort Simpson with a more favourable one is one such "irregularity." Clearly the Catholic bishop, Bishop Breynat, had a strong influence on Dene and is credited by Conroy, the Indian agent, with playing an influential role.

The treaty itself is typical of such documents, but history and legalism have made particular words and phrases very important. In broad strokes, what the state got out of the treaty was a clause that read "Dene hereby cede, release, convey and surrender all their rights, titles and interests to lands within the following bounds" and goes on to describe the overall territory of Denendeh. The treaty also included promises by the Dene to be law-abiding citizens (the language of which, as legal scholar Sakej Henderson has noted, involves commitments to act as law preservers, implying some degree of self-governing powers). Dene were promised reserve lands, school houses, annual hunting, trapping, and fishing supplies; the right to pursue their usual avocations of hunting, trapping, and fishing; annual gifts of money and one-time, slightly larger payments of cash; supplies, flags, medals, and clothing.

Two things about the written record are particularly worthy of note. First, the official report and papers from the Treaty 11 negotiations have disappeared and have never been recovered. Second, in an area of history and law where every detail is subject to intense reading, it is significant that the surrender clause specifies "land" but not water. The corresponding clause in the modern Sahtu Treaty, on the other hand, carefully surrenders title to "lands and waters."

It became clear soon after Treaty 11 was negotiated that Dene did not look favourably on the idea of reserves. They rightly thought that reserves would confine them to one area of land and make the hunting fishing trapping lifestyle more difficult, as happened in southern jurisdictions. So they resisted attempts to set up reserves. Since doing so in the north would have involved some expense at the best of times, and since no "oil rush" developed nor any other significant influx of newcomer-settlers, reserves were not established. A formal treaty promise documented in the text of the treaty was violated.

In the late '50s the state asked the question: Why are there no reserves in the NWT? A commission, eventually called the Nelson Commission after its chair, was set up to investigate the issue. The investigation apparently included travelling to the Dene villages

Cho and taking testimony. The commission re-
had seen reserves as little more than prisons and
"confined" on them. Remarkably, for the com-
eared that Dene had not thought they had surren-
dered their title to the land. Furthermore, the commission reported
that Dene still felt that way and any attempt to establish them on
reserves would create unrest and distress, which the commission
recommended against.

It is important to recognize that Dene were not, for the most
part, opposed to the treaty itself. In fact, I have heard many Dene
elders speak eloquently and passionately about the importance of the
treaty relationship. They think of the treaty as a document that establishes a relationship based on mutual respect, and not as a land
surrender. Hence, when they often insist on upholding the treaty, it is
this relationship they want upheld, not the element of land surrender.

A little more than a decade after the Nelson Commission, the
chiefs behind the newly organized Indian Brotherhood of the NWT,
which would evolve into the Dene Nation, sent representatives who
entered the office of the NWT land registrar and presented him with
a legal application for a "land caution," claiming that they still had
unsurrendered Aboriginal title to the whole of Denendeh (the NWT
at that time included what is now the territory of Nunavut). The
land registrar, good bureaucrat that he was, turned the issue over
to the Superior Court of the NWT, headed at that time by Justice
Morrow. Morrow had followed in the outstanding footsteps of his
predecessor, Justice Sissons, in using a "circuit court" approach to
the administration of justice: basically this meant taking the court
to each of the communities in lengthy, sometimes quite difficult,
but very important trips. Both Sissons and Morrow, having spent
time in Dene, Metis, and Inuit communities, had developed strong
sympathies with Indigenous peoples, and in many respects their

legal thinking on Aboriginal rights and titles was ahead of the thinking of other jurists in Canada.

Morrow decided to pay particularly close attention to Dene oral history, anticipating an approach that the Supreme Court of Canada would adopt about two decades later. The federal government attempted the unprecedented step of trying to use one federal court to block the proceedings of another, predictably failing. Morrow's concern to render a fair decision led him to a variety of Dene villages and into the homes of the more infirm of the elders in order to get direct testimony regarding the treaty. Much of this testimony provided the substance for René Fumoleau to write his *As Long as This Land Shall Last: A History of Treaty 8 and Treaty 11*, the most detailed study of these treaties and a pathbreaking venture in Indigenous oral history. Morrow observed the problems with the *X* marks, recorded the issue of selective leadership in Fort Simpson, and found other problems. Most Dene appear not to have been told about the land surrender or extinguishment clause on the document they were signing (when they actually signed). They were told, elder after elder insisted, that it was a treaty of peace and friendship and that they would be given gifts and help for "sharing the land," not for surrendering it. In a decision called *Re: Paulette*, named after the first of the chiefs who signed the original application (Francois Paulette from Fort Smith), a decision that would ultimately be one of the most important in Morrow's career, Morrow held in favour of the Dene applicants and directed the land registrar to file and apply their injunction.

Since at this time the Mackenzie Valley pipeline project was on the table, the federal government could not afford to allow such a claim to stand. Morrow's decision was quickly overturned. But in 1973, when the decision was handed down, the Supreme Court of Canada was also changing history in its famous *Calder* decision (especially through Emmet Hall's justifiably highly regarded dissenting opinion) regarding Nisga'a title to their traditional territories in the Nass River valley of British Columbia. Aboriginal rights and Aboriginal title were returning to the Canadian legal landscape. *Re: Paulette* (1973) played a role in this return. As a result of the *Calder* case in particular, the federal government realized that Aboriginal title, where unsurrendered, had legal force. The government (re)established a comprehensive land claims process for negotiating contemporary treaties, setting up an office in 1974. This was the start of the negotiations that would lead to the Dene/Metis agreement in principle of 1989 and the Sahtu Treaty of 1994. I have been told that one of the signatories of the land injunction application was the chief of Fort Norman (Tulita), Paul Wright. One of the names on Treaty 11 from Fort Norman was that of his uncle, Albert Wright.

Albert Wright

In my time with Begade Shutagot'ine much was said about Treaty 11. There was a palpable sense of respect for the relationship established through treaty and a sense, found in many other Indigenous communities, that all of the things offered by government—school buildings, medical services, social assistance, housing—were provided as treaty entitlements. There was also a sense of pride involved in the notion that the treaty established sharing the land, as opposed to extinguishment, the latter approach was seen as an attempt by newcomers simply to unjustly "take" all of the land. Extinguishment represented an attribute of human beings despised by Begade Shutagot'ine though not entirely unfamiliar to them, especially in this world where that attribute governs as the ruling principle of our time: greed.

Begade Shutagot'ine know about greed the same as many peoples do. They have to teach their children to share; neither greed or sharing are inherent (at least, in my view), but certainly sharing is a valued attribute that needs to be instilled, embodied. Generous people are respected as leaders among Begade Shutagot'ine, as among other Dene of Denendeh, as among other gathering and hunting or bush peoples around the world. Rapacious people, who eagerly take more than they can ever possibly hope to use, are the leaders of the Western world in our age, which widely admires unprecedented levels of unmitigated avarice. For Begade Shutagot'ine, such avarice in adults is child-like behaviour, implies immaturity, and signals weakness, poor socialization. In my view, this is one of the key reasons why Begade Shutagot'ine can be characterized as a more "advanced" people than the majority of humans in this world in this time, and certainly more than those in the countries most closely associated with "progress."

Albert Wright's name is on Treaty 11. But there is some question as to whether it belongs there. Apparently, he was one of the few Dene children sent off to a residential school in Montreal in their youth. There, he learned enough about Western literacy to be able to write his name. His name is signed on documents pertaining to certain lands in the Mackenzie Mountains. He was proud of the fact that he could "properly" sign his proper name. On Treaty 11, beside the name of Albert Wright, sits an *X*.

It seems that Albert Wright knew enough to be concerned about Dene lands possibly being stolen. Perhaps his time in Montreal gave him some insight into the avarice of the newcomers. In order to save that portion of the land that was most precious to him, my Begade friends and teachers Paul and Gabe and David kept insisting to me, Albert had "put up some posts." "What kinds of posts?" I wondered. "They're still there," they would say, "still up at Caribou Flats. When you go up there you'll see them." This became one of my goals, to see what kinds of posts they were. My mind raced—"Some kind of Dene version of a totem pole?" I speculated, in spite of the improbability. So great is the hold of certain images on our imaginations that even I, who certainly ought to have known better, had such ideas. Whatever the posts were, if they could still be seen, I would make whatever effort needed to be made to see them.

As a leader of Begade Shutagot'ine, Albert Wright had left some kind of marker on the land to insist upon Begade Shutagot'ine rights or title to the territories of his people. A document existed, Treaty 11, which purported to have his signature on it and purported to surrender Begade Shutagot'ine title to their lands. Another kind of document had been constructed, a document inscribed upon and an intimate part of the lands in question, by one of the great and humble leaders of the people. That document, a physical material gesture, an embodied writing, still existed, still insisted on the people's inalienable right to the territories they and their ancestors had occupied since time before time before memory, before before before.

Albert Wright, from the time of history and memory and myth. Historied by the narrative of Treaty 11. Remembered by his nephew and others who knew him as a "man of flesh and blood." Mythed by me and others who heard the stories. Albert Wright, whose signature would not be allowed to stand for surrender in the Begade Shutagot'ine annals of their own history. Albert Wright, whose writing abilities included writing on the paper and writing on the land, who knew many ways of signing himself.

Albert Wright was Begade Shutagot'ine.

History Repeats Itself

One of the most famous comments of nineteenth-century philosophy belongs to Karl Marx, who wrote that "Hegel remarks somewhere that all the great events and characters of world history occur, so to speak, twice. He forgot to add: the first time as tragedy, the second as farce" (1974). From Hegel to Marx to Nietzsche, an impressive trilogy of philosophers with widely divergent political views whose time spans what is now called the long nineteenth century, there is a notion

of historical repetition (which of course can be traced back to earlier historical moments in Western and other traditions of thought).
In our times, such a notion is taken up by the intellectual historian
Dominick LaCapra in his astute, elegant, and rigorous discussions of
the voluminous and expanding studies of the Shoah. For LaCapra,
repetition parallels what Freud called repetition-compulsion in certain kinds of neuroses; LaCapra suggests that such repetition involves
avoidance of the difficult "working through" that must be engaged in
when faced with historical trauma. Repetition-compulsion is a kind
of weakness; in the historical register perhaps it in part has to do with
a refusal of history itself, the refusal to learn to face difficult history
(those who do not learn from history are condemned to repeat it is
the now banal formulation). For LaCapra, working through is not
an easily determined, step-by-step process. It has a certain mystery,
involving as it does another kind of repetition (though the anthro-
pologist Michael Taussig [1987] would likely insist the repetition of
"working through" need not be as carefully calibrated and controlled
as LaCapra argues).

In 1921 a document appeared that purported to extinguish the
land rights of the Begade Shutagot'ine and other Dene to their traditional territories. In 1994 a document appeared that purported to
extinguish the land rights of the Begade Shutagot'ine to their traditional territories. The language in the two documents of this purported extinguishment is very nearly exactly the same. The injustice
of the purported extinguishment is also very nearly exactly the same.
In this instance of historical repetition, both events contain elements
of tragedy and of farce.

In 1921 a chief probably did not sign the document that bears
an X purporting to be his signature. Instead of surrendering his land,
he responded to the document by going out of his way to re-inscribe
the lands in question with markers of ownership rights.

In 1994 a relation of that same chief did not sign the document that does not purport to have his signature. He did not enrol as a beneficiary. Instead of surrendering his land, he signed a petition and several other letters and documents that insisted on his continued Aboriginal rights to the lands in question and in this way re-inscribed the lands in question with markers of ownership rights.

The extinguishment clause was used in treaty documents from at least the time of the Robinson Treaties (1850) through to the Sahtu Treaty (1994). The treaties that followed 1994 actually use language that in many respects is worse (what I have called the "exhaustion" clause). The "principle" behind all this language is benignly called "certainty," and this principle is what underwrites the contemporary treaty process. Certainly, it can be said, the accumulation of capital requires certainty. Whether people require it is another matter. My activist friend Russell Diabo insists that what certainty amounts to can be thought of as, very simply, "termination."

In the late nineteenth and early twentieth centuries, learned lawyers believed they could articulate in a document principles that would stand the test of time and last "as long as the sun shines and the grasses grow and the river runs." The actual wording of these documents was in some respects outdated within a few decades: for example, the five-dollar annuity over the decades lost its value as a significant contribution to Indigenous family economies. The principles of land surrender, while working well for the avaricious newcomers, did not stand the test of time for Indigenous signatories, for the most part reducing them to the state of immiserated occupants of small patches of land on their traditional territories. The learned lawyers were wrong, astoundingly so. They did not have the skills to see into the future. Instead of trying to establish a relationship that could evolve, they locked into legal documents a limited vision of property relations.

In the late twentieth century we are still living with this legal hubris, practised every day by very well-paid staff of the euphemistically named "justice department." The Begade Shutagot'ine are supposed to pay the price of the pride of these officials—as they did in 1921. In 1994 they refused.

Canadians would rather ignore or forget about the "sad history" of our treatment of the Indigenous inhabitants of this land. It's best to turn this page on the past. Let bygones be bygones. We can't undo what's been done. Get on with it, live in the present. These convenient sentiments circulate informally in living-room consciences, and formally in the writings of cheerleaders of capitalist progress the ilk of Thomas Flanagan on the political right or Frances Widdowson on the political, er, right. As they wave their pompoms ever more frantically in the vain hope of convincing us that these ideas are new and haven't formed the basis of 100 years of disastrous policy making, it is worth reminding ourselves that such forgetting dooms us to continue the same process, the same results. It could even be seen as funny, if it were not in fact so acutely, painfully tragic.

A Petition

In their attempt to prevent Begade Shutagot'ine lands from being taken away from them, Paul and Gabe had organized a petition among their people who lived in Tulita. Pretty much every one of the Begade Shutagot'ine adults signed it. This in spite of the fact that feelings were strong and those who supported the treaty put pressure on others to support it. There was talk of jobs being denied to people because they had signed the petition or, later, because they would not sign up as beneficiaries. Clarence Campbell, the bright young man who had introduced me to Paul and acted as our first translator at the Dehcho Assembly, was under a great deal of stress over these issues: his opportunities to find good office-based work that he was qualified for were mitigated by his respect for Paul and his knowledge of the principles involved. He had a young family to feed and a future at stake. Driving around town with me, he agonized about his choices. Those who worked for the Sahtu secretariat, I was told, had been going from house to house instructing people that they had to participate in the vote. It's hard to know how much of this is truth, but these are some of the things I was told by Paul and Gabe and David, all reliable sources, so I believe them.

I talked to some of the younger Dene politicians, who knew about Paul's stand and said he had "lost touch" with things, that he was "out of step" with the times. They expressed admiration for him in a general way but thought that he was now playing an obstructive role. Later, when young Dene led a charge against the newly proposed Mackenzie Valley gas project, they were dismissed by the same leaders as too "young and idealistic." Fortunate indeed is the generation that can tack skilfully between these dangerous poles: the out-of-touch elders and the idealistic youth.

A vote had been held in the five Sahtu communities regarding the then-proposed Sahtu Treaty in the summer of 1994. I was in Fort Good Hope at the time and knew little about what was going on in Tulita. I did know that Colville Lake had formally requested they be allowed a community-by-community vote, with communities given the opportunity to opt out if they so voted. This eminent and sensible plan was entirely rejected. The Begade Shutagot'ine had wanted the same thing, and had also been rebuffed.

Two other issues around the process emerged. One was that the vote would take place in a mere few months after the draft settlement; people were given relatively little time to understand a complex legal document that would have an impact on their future, forever. A second issue regarded the fact that the "information sessions" established to provide people with knowledge about the proposed treaty were conducted by Dene and Metis negotiators of the treaty whose interest was in a positive vote; hence these sessions became sales pitches for the treaty and there was no support for debate, no support for anyone who wanted to speak against the proposed treaty. The "sellers" were paid to do that work and were paid expenses for their travel and had pamphlets and maps to give out. Paul Wright had his own limited financial resources (almost nonexistent, really) and, as did others, expressed his concerns on his own time, working entirely out of a sense of principle and commitment to the future of his people. Such a dynamic has been repeated endlessly in Indian country. Jobs, money, and resources for those who want to sell the deal; expense, lost time, pressure, and agonizing decisions for those who have concerns, doubts, or criticisms. Paul Wright's problem was aggravated by the complexity of the principled stand he was taking: he did not advocate rejection of the deal itself ("if the other communities wanted to have this deal, they should have it, they have the right to decide for themselves" would paraphrase his position) but rather that the deal not be applied to Begade Shutagot'ine people or lands.

The federal government's rejection of proposals for a community-by-community vote in the Sahtu is interesting. In the late 1970s, the federal government had insisted that Metis and Dene negotiate one global land claim for the whole of Denendeh. They did not want overlapping claims and they did not want splinter claims. A decade later, when Dene requested reopening negotiations around the global agreement in principle (AIP) over treaty rights and extinguishment, they were rejected. When the Gwich'in, under enormous pressure from feeling they were falling behind nearby Inuvialuit peoples who had settled a modern treaty, walked out of the Dene Assembly and proposed a regional land claim, the federal government eagerly set up a negotiation table for them and settled a regional agreement, based on the AIP, within a year. The Sahtu

came from the next region, following the Gwich'in settlement. Who belongs in the Sahtu and who doesn't? Who has the
power to determine which borders would be fixed and determinate,
and which would be flexible and shift with time? In this case, it is
clear that the federal government had and used such power, always
in the interest of getting signatures on land surrenders.

The vote was held in the summer of 1993, and passed by a healthy
majority of 85 percent of Dene voters and 99 percent of Metis voters. Many Begade Shutagot'ine boycotted: they did not want to vote
"no" and risk losing the treaty for those in the other communities
who were anxious to pass it. Their principles hurt their own future.
But they felt that the leaders, the minister and officials of Indian
Affairs, were honourable people who would have to take their concerns into account. The minister herself, then Pauline Browes, travelled to Tulita for the signing ceremony for the Sahtu Treaty. At least
there is some sense of the historical importance of these agreements
in the highest offices, which there hadn't been in 1921. Tulita is a
small town and there was no way for the minister to avoid Begade
Shutagot'ine even if she wanted to. It's unlikely, though, that she had
any sense of the conflict that was shaping their entire future. The petition was passed to the minister. Since it was a ceremonial time, no
one expected her to look at it or do anything in particular about it.

Tulita is a small town and there was no way for the minister
to avoid Begade Shutagot'ine even if she wanted to. It's unlikely,
though, that she had any sense of the conflict that was shaping their
entire future. Furthermore, the member of Parliament for the area, a
junior minister in her own government who travelled with her, was
Ethel Blondin-Andrew, who was connected by marriage to Begade
Shutagot'ine and looked up to Paul Wright as a friend and adviser.
She herself made introductions. The petition was passed to the minister. Since it was a ceremonial time, no one expected her to look at
it or do anything in particular about it. But she received it in person

with the usual assurances that the matter would be looked into. The last Paul saw of it—the document with all those signatures, each one representing an agonizing choice, each name a trace of the pride in being able to stand up to the overwhelming forces of the established order, the whole a profound statement of principle by Begade Shutagot'ine—it had been folded and tucked into the inside upper pocket of the minister's suit jacket. As distinct from these careful words and names, each forged in the smithy of principle and pride, each traced with great deliberation and caution, each the subject of careful thought, as distinct from these the hollowness of the words they evoked in response: "They would look into it."

Tulita

The town of Tulita is a typical small Dene village, located on the south bank of the Sahtu Deh where it flows into the Deh Cho and stretching southward along the east side of that great river. It started, as was the case with many villages, as a fishing camp that evolved into a fur trading post called Fort Norman, and was among the earlier of the Dene communities to reappropriate its name. It's a lovely little town, with many of the houses running on both sides of the main road that runs parallel to the high bank along the Deh Cho. On the north side of the Sahtu Deh is Bear Rock, perhaps one of the most well-known sacred sites of the Dene, in part because a representation of it is used as the Dene Nation logo. There aren't many amenities in Tulita: when I worked there with Paul and Gabe there was no hotel, so I had to billet with Paul or with the Etchinelle family, often at Michael Widow's house. There was no restaurant. For public facilities there was a newish school, a new band office building, and an older nursing station. The old Anglican church in town was run-down and hardly used; the Roman Catholic church was in a somewhat better state of repair; a newer Pentecostal facility was outfitted with a satellite dish, so I had the sense of a broadcast-based religion. There was a small northern store in town, less well-stocked than most of the Northern stores across Denendeh; people often made boat or, in winter, winter-road trips to Norman Wells, the next and substantially larger town downriver for big grocery shopping binges or for big-ticket items. Sometimes people would drive down to Hay River or even Edmonton for the latter.

The major event of most evenings was radio bingo. In the late afternoon many people could be seen scurrying here and there, picking up and delivering bingo cards. It always seemed so benign to me that I could never associate bingo with the epithet of gambling, but I guess it was that. You daren't attempt to use anyone's telephones while the bingo numbers are being called; if you are at the house of a winner they would need the phone to call in their win. Hence, even trying to make a social call during bingo hour is a perilous, difficult-to-impossible venture. On the other hand, bingo hour is a good time to hang out with the "guys" and make the drive from one end of town to the next, chatting with and visiting whomever you run into, being as bad as you can afford to be.

During the period of this study I was frequently in Tulita. My time there was often rewarding in its own right. For my first two visits to Paul, Tulita was the final destination: David Etchinelle would pick me up by boat from Pehdzeh Ki to the south or Norman Wells to the north. In a third year we passed through Tulita for a few days on our way to Caribou Flats, flying directly into Tulita on the scheduled flight from Yellowknife. The following summer we passed through again, on our way to Drum Lake, spending a few days there. My next two visits to Begade Shutagot'ine were to Tulita and didn't involve getting out on the land. The summer I met Paul I was travelling with my then partner Elizabeth Fajber. She also made the first of my trips to Tulita with me. We had decided to go our separate ways by the time of the trip to Caribou Flats. My research assistant on that trip,

Kimberly Harkness, was an undergraduate student who is still remembered by Begade Shutagot'ine for her work ethic. By the time I travelled to Drum Lake I was with a new partner, Krista Pilz, and another research assistant, Jim Welch. The last two trips were made on my own. Years later as I write this in Kolkata, Krista and I have also parted. And I've made many more trips to Tulita, to go over this manuscript with the Etchinelles, to help them continue Paul and Gabe's struggle. My daughter Malay now sometimes comes along—and is a very useful researcher in her own right!—as do more research assistants: Agnes Pawlowska, Emily Grafton, Les Sabiston, and my partner for a brief period, the artist Jaime Drew (more widely known as Jaime Black). So the world turns and somehow I manage not to get knocked off. I remember reading Claude Lévi-Strauss's famous *Tristes Tropiques*, a great book, and being struck by the fact that somewhere around page 300 he mentions in an offhand way that his wife was travelling with him; the implication was that she was there all along, but from the text the reader never knew it until that one mention. So I feel it somehow important to set this part of my record straight, however poorly it reflects on my abilities as a relationship sustainer: I did learn a great deal from all the various partners and research assistants I worked with on this project. More to the point, I learned a lot from Tulita.

There are people I met only in Tulita: Morris Mendo, an older, kindly man who worked for the church and was close to Paul. Michael Widow, who always had a steady wage job and owned the jet boat we used, but didn't have the time himself to go on many of the trips. I often stayed with him, or with Rosa Etchinelle. In the later period my good friend Deborah Lee Simmons lived there, so that would entail at least a visit. I usually visited with Clarence Campbell, who was closer to me in age and interests. Others, like Chief Frank Andrew, some of the Metis Hardisty family, or the elder Elizabeth Yakelia, I made brief acquaintance with. There is much more to Tulita than the Begade Shutagot'ine; it is a fascinating community in its own right. In my time there, because of the kind of work I was doing and because of the political drama unfolding around the Sahtu Treaty, the division between Willow Lake people and Begade Shutagot'ine seemed somewhat more acute than perhaps it usually was. I would not want to leave readers with the impression of a town divided. In most instances, around most issues, and in the practice of cultural activities that bespoke the fact of community, Dene of all sorts and Metis in Tulita were in accord.

Tulita had many gifts of many kinds to offer. One time as I walked back along the gravel road on the high banks of the Deh Cho in the shadow of Bear Rock in the dusk of the late gathering darkness, past the nursing station and past the Pentecostal church, not quite at Morris Mendo's house, where there are no houses on the Deh Cho side of the road, something large and grey glided silently by me, flying westwards toward the river toward the nearly completely setting sun, flying directly before me and only a few feet above my head. While my day was nearly done, while I was off to my room to rest and read, perhaps chat a bit with David or Paul, owl's long night of hunting had just begun.

A Drum Dance in Tulita

In the summer of 1995 something quite extraordinary happened. A fire had been raging on the east side of the Deh Cho, slowly working its way up to Tulita. It was a huge bush fire and there was never any question of trying to put it out. The hope was that it would burn itself out before it reached any of the communities. As the fire got closer to Tulita, though, it was clear that the whole town was in danger. So there was an evacuation order, and the people were airlifted and boated out. A team of firefighters stayed in town to do what could be done, save what could be saved. The fire burned straight up the Deh Cho from the south, but some few hundreds metres before Tulita a shift in the wind caused it to abruptly change direction and burn eastwards, inland, a little ways before returning to its northward trajectory. It was just enough of a shift to save the town of Tulita: almost as if the fire made a deliberate box turn around the town. The only damage from the fire was to a small shed near the airport, which was lit ablaze and burned to the ground by sparks carried on the wind. When the fire was safely north of the community the people returned, and within a day or so of that event, I reached town myself.

The community decided to hold a drum dance to honour the firefighters who had stayed to protect the community. Many of these were from other places. One of the striking things about Tulita in the years I visited was the vitality of the culture of the Dene drum. There were frequent drum dances, every few nights, and a very active drum group. In most of the Dene communities I have been to, drummers would come out on special occasions, but there were sometimes barely enough of them to pull together a strong, consistent, well-rehearsed group. The Tulita drummers are well-known, often singing some of the many songs apparently composed in a burst of creative energy by old man Andrew, the leader of the Andrew clan in the old days. Certainly Begade Shutagot'ine played a major part in the drum group, which was often led by Frank Andrew. David Etchinelle also consistently helped lead the group. Although the two would later have serious political differences, they could always be found together, committed to teaching the young people about Dene ways, never worrying about the fact that they were never paid a cent for these daily efforts.

The firefighters' drum dance was scheduled to start at about eight o'clock in the community hall, a small, rectangular-shaped building in "downtown" Tulita. Of course, things actually started much later; life operated on Dene time. The drummers slowly gathered, tried out a few songs while they were sitting. People were slowly drifting in and sitting along the bench that circled the long room. The drummers tried those few songs but everyone was shy about being the first to dance. Finally, as the drummers were feeling ready but no one was dancing, Frank, a social-convener type of guy, came up to Elizabeth and me and suggested we try a "pick a partner" dance. While they drummed we would dance, when they called out we would each pick a new partner, when they called out again each would find someone else, and so on until everyone was dancing. This would kick-start the dancing: once people danced for a first time and broke the ice, there would be no trouble getting them to continue. So that's what we did. My first pick was a very young girl I had been playing with earlier, who had been quite outgoing with me as someone to tease but then was mortified when she saw me heading straight at her, though the elders forced her to follow the rule and do the bit of dancing with me. Once enough of us were out there the dancing gathered momentum. The drummers stood up anytime anyone danced, so they spent most of the rest of the evening on their feet.

Light lingers long on those northern summer days, but after dancing three or four or ten or twelve rounds—time and counting lose their linearity in the drum dance—darkness had risen from its depths and with its silent inevitability ruled the outdoors. I stepped outside for a break, to cool myself and let the sweat on my skin chill me, to stand with the cigarette smokers and join in the idle chat. A fire was burning in a barrel just outside of the community hall. Among the children running around on the outskirts of the drum dance, some would come at some sign from a drummer and take the drum from him, or take several that were passed down the line of drummers, running it out to someone who stood by the fire and running in with fire-dried replacements. As these "new" drums were passed from hand to hand, mid-song, along the line of drummers, the force of the fresh drums would be renewed and drummers and dancers would be charged with a new intensity. So the songs and drums and dances ebbed and flowed long into the night, as the drum group waxed or waned from eight or nine drummers to four or five, as the drums themselves grew tired and were fire-refreshed.

At some point there was a pause. Chief Frank Andrew said a few eloquent words of praise, thanking the firefighters for their work and their courage, and showing gratitude that the community had been spared. The firefighters then led the circle in the next dance for the next song, and the dance continued. Many, perhaps most, community members were there, packing the tiny hall. To poor dancers like me, there is not much to see in the rhythmic shuffle of feet to drums; but I noticed at some point many of the women jostling for position behind a young man from Deline who was, I heard some of those who had danced behind him saying, dancing in the old style. So I watched his feet, trying to figure out what was different. I asked a nearby young woman I knew. She said, "Can't you see? Watch his feet! They never touch the ground."

We left the dance sometime close to two in the morning. It was going strong, and according to later reports lasted until five or six, not unusual in summer. Dene well know how to celebrate the lives they have been given. With the simple tools of drums and voices, feet and fire, they weave a complex and magical tapestry where joy friendship passion have wings, where the sacred bonds of community itself shatter the possibility of spectacle and take flight, where intensity and exhaustion, endurance and ease circle each other soaring ever higher, where even a stranger can feel the electric shock of what it is to be alive. Even alive for merely a brief moment. Alive in this world that only desires dead samenesses. A drum dance in Tulita is not a thing to behold. It is a thing to embody.

Elizabeth Yakelia

This too is a story I've told elsewhere, in an article called "From Appropriation to Subversion." It belongs here, though, as well.

At the drum dance for the firefighters we noticed at some point a very elderly Dene woman wagging a finger at some small children. I imagined that she was chastising them for running around inside the building while the dancing and drumming was taking place, but she could just as easily have been saying something like "Now if you come and visit me tomorrow I'll give you some nice chocolates!" There was no way of knowing, but her talking to the children caused me to take notice of her.

Much later in the night, well after midnight, she went to the drummers as they conferred about what song they would play next. They then lined up to play her request; she stood beside them, almost invisible, she was so slight and hunched over, and the male drummers and drums so large with such a commanding physical presence. But her head was twisted upwards and she sang along with the drummers. I had never seen a woman singing at any of the many drum dances I had attended, so this stood out starkly, though no one from Tulita paid any mind; everyone danced as always. I was later told that she was from Willow Lake and wanted an old Willow Lake song, rather than the Begade Shutagot'ine songs that were the stock-in-trade of the drummers. It was just another unusual event, another thing to place in the file of memory-gifts from Tulita, something new to ponder.

That was our last day in Tulita on that trip; Elizabeth and I were to travel by boat to Norman Wells the next day, late in the afternoon, staying overnight there to catch a morning flight back to the south. David couldn't get time off work to take us but arranged a ride with friends. We were to meet with them at someone named Elizabeth Yakelia's house. David described to us where the house was and with a bit of trepidation we went looking for it in the early afternoon. My fear was that the woman, an elder, I was told, wouldn't speak English, and if our contacts weren't there we might have a few confusing or uncomfortable moments. On the other hand, I was well used to those moments, so certainly wouldn't let fear of it slow or stop us.

We arrived at the house and walked in without knocking, in the Dene way. There was a long, dark, narrow hall, and the woman was home. She came to greet us when she heard the door open, somewhat surprised to see two *mola*, no doubt. Elizabeth Yakelia proved to be none other than the female elder we had seen talking to the children and singing the night before. She did indeed speak English. Slavey. French. And a bit of Latin as well. Her language skills, it turned out, were vastly superior to my own. There was no question of either confusion or discomfort. She was a gracious, considerate Dene host. She was pleased with the coincidence of her own and Elizabeth Fajber's names, and we could have happily spent endless hours with her, drinking tea and chatting. She was an astute, articulate conversationalist. It wasn't long before she started to root around, looking for suitable gifts to present to her visitors. She soon found a St. Christopher's medal, knowing we were to travel later that day. She also presented us with a coffee mug that bore a photograph of Pope John Paul II. It was Dene spirituality as embodied in the giving of gifts, here folded over commodified Catholic religion: icons of the church configured as Dene-style gifts. We had nothing to offer in return but our visit itself, which she appeared to enjoy as much as we did.

Later that day we were on the river again, Tulita receding into the distance; but something of Elizabeth's generosity, her spirit, her kindness, her expressive powers, the issues we discussed—some of this stayed with us for the hours and days that followed, and perhaps even until and past this very moment of inscription. As with Tulita, which is always with me.

DEPOSITION TWO
Caribou Flats

Old voices echo; the ancient poetic memory of our ancestors finds home in our individual lives and allows us to reshape our experience so that we can interpret the world we find ourselves in.
—NEAL MCLEOD

The river is like a genealogy—in fact, it *is* a genealogy in a very concrete way, considering how many members of my family live on both sides of the river. It is like a genealogy also in that at the specific place I consider my home, there is always both an upstream, the river that comes before, and a downstream, the river that comes after.
—RAUNA KUOKKANEN

Into the Mountains

After meeting Paul Wright and Gabe Etchinelle during one year and, having acquired a research grant to work with them, visiting them in Tulita during the next year, it was time to travel with them into the mountains. That time was August 1997. I had spent July on Baffin Island, the first year of the summer school I founded in Pangnirtung. After about a week in the south, I was ready to return to Denendeh, knowing that August was a good time to be travelling into the Mackenzie Mountains. With me was my student, Kimberly

Harkness, whose work ethic and wide range of talents convinced me she would make a suitable research assistant on the trip. Another professor, Julia Harrison, joined us as far as Tulita but returned before we went into the mountains. By my use of "we" in these passages I refer to all who made this journey.

We would travel in two jet boats. One involved the Etchinelle family, Theresa and David, with their sons James, David Jr., and the youngest, Tyler. The other boat involved Leon Andrew, his brother Paul Andrew, two of their nephews, and Paul and Gabe. Kimberly and I rounded out the group. Before the trip, James and I had travelled partway upriver to drop off a barrel of fuel; various caches of fuel had already been planted at strategic locations. As we left Tulita heading south on the Deh Cho, I noticed that we weren't carrying many groceries, even fewer than usual on trips where the hunters expected the land to provide. We'd make do with what we hunted, I guessed.

Before leaving Tulita, Kimberly and I, following Theresa's advice, "fed the river"—making an offering of bundled willows in the hopes of a successful journey, in the manner of Dene.

We travelled two days, first south on the Deh Cho, then west and north on the Begade. We therefore camped for a night en route. They were long days of travel. The Deh Cho portion of the trip was nondescript as we moved against its mighty, sluggish current. The roar of the powerful engines made conversation while travelling nearly impossible save for a few shouted fragments and phrases.

The Begade was another matter altogether. It was not nearly as wide as the Deh Cho, and its water was clearer. It was shallow and split into all kinds of channels, many so small that for our purposes they were dead ends. And gravel bottomed, as its name indicated. The drivers, experienced as they were, still had to be alert constantly. The main channel would shift from year to year, so one had to know the river but also be able to judge the moment, its current state. The jet boats could cross very shallow stretches of water, even with the load of all the people and gear in these boats, but used extraordinary amounts of fuel, each carrying a few forty-five-gallon barrels of gas, which would all be used. It was cold on the Deh Cho, cool on the Begade, especially when the sun disappeared behind mountains, behind clouds, or when it sprinkled a bit of rain, as it often did on that trip.

Slowly, as we went up the Begade, we left behind the undulating bush landscape of that part of the Deh Cho and were embraced and surrounded by mountains. We passed Red Dog Mountain and left an offering of some bullets and tobacco to acknowledge its sacred nature. The mountains of the Begade are limestone based and show layers of colour, which to the casual observer make for long twisting dancing lines of orange and red and yellow that would crash against the river and smile down at its many sandbars.

We would stop and make tea or cook a fish, eating it right off a pile of fresh-cut leaves with a bit of salt. We would stop and visit a tourist camp, where the owners treated these mountain Dene respectfully, offering good hospitality with a few curious looks thrown the way of these whites who travelled with them. We would stop and walk into a bit of nondescript bush to pick up another gas drum left there by snowmobiles in the spring for this purpose, feeling the heavy weight of it as we rolled it out and delicately manoeuvred it into the boat. We would stop and be told that from this point we could see the break in the trees that marked the Canol pipeline, which Paul had worked on as a guide many years ago. We would be shown this cabin as we passed and told that this is where the Simmons family had lived, more than a decade ago.

Then we would pile back into the boat, cover ourselves with sleeping bags, shift to find as comfortable a position as possible in whatever spot we had made for ourselves, and start again, continuing along in the long hours of travel upriver.

Travel itself helps to forge friendship or establish enmities. Where friendships are forged the story of the journey becomes a mutual one, life stories meeting up for however brief a period. Our Begade Shutagot'ine hosts quickly learned that both Kimberly and I were not going to complain about the cold the wet the long hours, or whatever else was inconvenient or conventionally uncomfortable (the toilet facilities!). We learned that our hosts were reliable and kindly and weren't going to allow us to suffer undue hardship, certainly nothing that couldn't be handled. I learned to respect the knowledge and skills of Begade Shutagot'ine. I learned something about the great beauty of their land.

Much of the Begade twists and turns through a broad valley, mountains in the distance on both sides, splits and splits and splits into islands and sandbars. Occasionally, the river cuts right up to the base of some small layered cliff at the foot of some mountain, usually winding around in a sharp about-face at that point, following the cliff for a stretch, and then leaving it for the softer landscape of the mid-valley. There were no major rapids or waterfalls for us to cross, though some stretches of broad shallow river had a lot of rolling water. There was a dramatic, steep-cut island with roiling water going around it called "the Steamboat" that we passed at some point, and a few other striking places. We were taken with the drama of the place, the colour, the ease, the beauty. It seemed to me, a canoeist of middling skill, to be an ideal river to canoe downstream: shallow, safe, many easy camp spots, not much used at that time by the canoe tourists. Every time I travel on the Begade I make an inevitable promise to come back on canoe, but it hasn't happened yet.

Our sense of ease with each other in the boats grew as the hours passed. The journey required some endurance, some patience. Slowly, as the mountains closed in around us, we came to know a little bit about each other; in my case I was really meeting Leon and Paul for the first time, and getting to know James and David Jr. and Tyler as well. Kimberly was meeting the whole gang, learning the story of the land claim, trying to catch up and learn how she could make herself useful.

Somehow I was expecting a particular site: we would arrive at some dramatic place and someone would announce, "We're at Caribou Flats!" and that would be that. In fact we stopped at a place, took a good look around, decided not to camp there for some reason I've forgotten, and moved on to another spot where they had apparently camped a few years before, deciding to stay there for some reason I've also forgotten. I, slow on the uptake, was thinking we were still on our way, and it was a few hours, I think, before I realized that this was now to be our base camp. We had arrived at Caribou Flats.

Boats were unloaded and tents set up. Two canvas-wall tents were set up for the groups in each of the two boats. Two small *mola* hiking tents were set up by Kimberly and me, nearer the river. Behind us was a long mountain ridge, with our little camp nestled at its feet. In front of us the Begade and a range of mountains that stretched as far as we could see in either direction along the river. There was a bit of clearing between the scrub spruce trees, as in any place that has been regularly "camped," and here and there were signs of previous Begade Shutagot'ine activity. Somehow, after the previous night when we simply unpacked the basics for a brief sleep, it felt a bit like luxury to unpack all the gear and set up the tent as a home for the next stretch of late summer days.

The air was clear. The daylight still lingered long into the evening. We drank the water fresh and cold out of the river. The mountains lay all around us with their inevitable promise of eternity, their weighty serenity, their heavy blank meaninglessness. We had two elders to tell us stories. We had many experienced hunters to find us meat. We had much to do, much to talk about. We were in the mountains and our days there were just beginning.

Paul Andrew and Leon Andrew

Paul and Leon were from another of the large Begade Shutagot'ine families, the Andrews. For much of the period when this study was undertaken, another of their siblings, Frank Andrew, was chief in Tulita. Paul has become one of the friends I make an effort to visit when I pass through Yellowknife, one of a circle of cosmopolitan Dene who might as easily be found walking the earth in Spain as butchering a caribou somewhere up the Begade. He is knowledgeable, gregarious, voluble, outgoing; easy to meet yet thoughtful and considerate. He was for many years the face of the major television newscast in Denendeh, *Focus North*, which is broadcast nationally through the Aboriginal People's Television Network; hence he was often recognized in Denendeh and certainly in "Indian country" across Canada.

Paul had longed for some time to return to the mountains he had spent so much time in as a youth and young man, and our planned trip afforded him a welcome opportunity. He timed his holiday to match our venture and helped to provide gas money for the boat he travelled with. He would aid me considerably, both by explaining what he knew of the Begade Shutagot'ine situation, which was quite a lot, and by translating, especially for Gabe. We remain in regular contact as friends. Years later, during "the troubles" at Trent University, the then chancellor of Trent, Peter Gzowski, had a lunch in Yellowknife with Paul during which my name came up. Paul hastened to assure Peter what a fine chap I was; since Gzowski was officially bound to the opposite political pole of our Trent battle, he could only shake his head sorrowfully: "Oh no," he said.

It took a little more time to get to know Leon, who was quieter. He chose his thoughtful words carefully, and also took care to point out or emphasize when something significant was being said or taking place to ensure Kimberly or I didn't miss it, such as when he told me what Gabe had told him about the tree where the bear gets its power. In Denendeh I wish to be taken for who I am rather than what I am said to be, and I try to treat others in the same manner. I found Leon to be kindly, knowledgeable, strong, and typically Dene-style easygoing. He too became a friend, one whom I see less often but whose company I enjoy in those rare times when I do find it.

In their beloved mountains, Begade Shutagot'ine shine as if lit by an inner fire. They are in their element, all at ease peace joy, emotions nurtured by a work and a play that fold over into each other. Paul Andrew and Leon Andrew are Begade Shutagot'ine.

Caribou Flats

What is it about certain places that call, that tug, that pull, that instill an almost physical longing? The hunting grounds at Caribou Flats are like that: bush river mountain country. Views that could make my heart ache just from looking. An easy terrain to negotiate. The kind of terrain that allows your feet to reward your eyes: any walk upwards would reveal magnificent vistas.

One day James led Kimberly and me and David Jr. up a small mountain on the other side of the river from our camp. We hadn't spotted any game after a few days and hoped that by climbing up we might find some just over the ridge, or be in a position to spot caribou or sheep from the higher vantage. We walked over the rounded stones of an old, nearly dried-up creek bed, slowly working upwards. Then we cut through some spruce and pines to the foot of the ridge. At last we began to work our way directly upwards, hiking up to terrain clear of trees, steep tiring slopes. As I walked up I kept my attention on the footing in front of me, too exhausted by each step to do much else, too determined not to falter. Eventually we crested the ridge and could stop and sit. Spread out before us was the Begade, the whole valley, mountains, our boat and camp; a stunning panorama.

We didn't get any sheep or caribou that day; didn't even see any. We came down empty-handed but—at least in my case—with a full spirit. I had seen something worth seeing.

There were a few days of not getting any big game, which led to some muttering. Perhaps the kids shouldn't be fishing, since Dene did not mix food from the water with food from the land, and this could be bringing us bad luck. Maybe my tent was too close to the river, too visible since it was brightly coloured. But, for hunters, Caribou Flats defies pessimism. We ended up hunting many caribou over the course of our time at the flats. One day, in the morning, the elders—with their eyes never far from the sheep trails that cut like thin threads across the mountains—spotted the small white slowly moving specks that were sheep, high up on the mountain behind us, and we went sheep hunting. We picked berries. Tyler hunted ground squirrels with a twenty-two-calibre rifle. At seemingly random stopping points we saw notched poles that had once been used to cache food high up in the trees. We were told about giant beavers that had once lived in these parts, that perhaps still could be found further upriver. Giant panthers too.

We worked hard, setting up camp, hunting and butchering and cooking and drying meat. But we also relaxed, breathing in the ease of camp life, drinking tea around the fire, trading stories of far-off lands, of times long past. The magic of clean air and clean water and wholesome food, the magic of being in the presence of strong kind elders worked its healing, material charms on us, gave us a feeling of well-being, gave us moments to sink in and feel like staying sunken forever. Paul and Gabe, especially, told stories of long walks into the mountain, of hunting trips where they would cross mountain after mountain with huge loads of game on their strong young shoulders, or where they would see their first African-Americans as soldiers with the U.S. Army, working together to build the Canol pipeline during the Second World War, or where they would cross the ranges and engage in hand games with Dene relatives from the Yukon, testing their powers against those of their distant neighbours; unbelievable feats of strength and endurance that they took for granted.

In this place where we could see so clearly, we could talk about Treaty 11 and the Sahtu Treaty and the Dehcho declaration and the personalities and politics of Denendeh. There was no rancour or ill will, but a determination, a clarity, a sense of purpose. In some ways this trip was for me, to show me these things, to teach, to instill a sense of what was at stake. In some ways this trip was for Paul and Leon and David and Theresa, to give them another chance at touching this piece of earth so precious to them and so central to their being. In some ways this trip was for Tyler and David Jr. and James and the other younger ones, to instill the meaning of Begade Shutagot'ine in their bodies and souls. In some ways this trip was for Paul and Gabe, to give them another opportunity at being the fullest selves they would always become when they nested in their mountains.

Hunting Caribou

What is it like to hunt caribou with Begade Shutagot'ine on their home grounds? This became our preoccupation in our first few days of camp life, leading to fruitless climbs, seemingly aimless meandering, and eventually, dramatic moments of success.

One time, we left by boat to search the shores for caribou. Along the west side of the river (we were camped on the east), not far upriver from our camp, on a creek bed, caribou were spotted. Kimberly and I were dropped off with Gabe and James. We were to work our way to a small stand of trees and bush. David, Theresa, and the kids went upstream in the boat, passing the caribou: their job was to drive the animals to us. As the boat left, we crouched behind some small willows. Gabe quickly cut a few branches and held them out to us to use for cover, holding them in front of us as we moved in a crouch across the sandspit to the stand of trees that was our destination. It was only at this point that I actually saw the caribou, a small herd in the distance. Then we waited. A few cigarettes later something was happening. David was running, almost in the very midst of the small herd. If he had a rifle he could have brought one down effortlessly. But his job was to scare. We had the rifles. A short distance after him were Theresa and the rest, also running and waving their arms and shouting. The caribou began to move. Instead of running across the clearing, along the river, right into our waiting arms, they had gotten some altogether foolish idea that going in another direction, further inland and away from us all, was the right thing to do. It was indeed the right thing to do, for them. It all happened so fast, and then they were gone: we didn't even get a chance at a shot. They were gone. The tension and excitement evaporated. We had a short walk back to the water's edge and another wait for the boat to return. The whole event took about forty minutes. The critical moments: less than five minutes. It takes about ten minutes to write it up, less than one minute to read. Empty hands, dangling.

One time, not long after this failed hunt, we were working our way upriver to another likely location of caribou when the boat swerved, changing direction. Caribou were climbing out of the river on the east side. They were easy to shoot in the river and as they came out: we got two so quickly I hardly knew what was happening. The hunters paid very little attention to the ones they had shot; their attention was focused on the caribou that had gotten into the trees, inland from the river. The boat quickly landed, the hunters were off into the bush. There's firewood to be gathered, a fire to light. Tea to be made. Caribou to be skinned and cut up. Ribs to be cooked. The caribou that went deeper into the bush escaped, but we had enough meat now for a few days or more. The taste of fresh ribs cooked over that small open fire still remains with me. What taste does the world offer that could be better?

Another time, perhaps the next day, we went upriver to the other spot we had been aiming at when our journey was interrupted as we found the caribou in the river. We arrived just downstream from a creek bed, climbed the high banks and peeked over fallen logs and through bush: a small herd of animals. Very quickly the hunters distributed themselves and identified which of the game would be their individual targets. The most powerful gun, with the best scope, would aim for the furthest viable animal. It would fire first with the others immediately following. All this was decided quickly, with gestures and whispers. From the time we left the boat to the first shot was probably less than three minutes. It felt like a meagre few heartbeats. Then the crack the roar of the rifles; impossible to absorb all that was happening, even from the excellent vantage point that I had; caribou crumpled caribou scattered into the trees, one with a shattered leg in pain and confusion splashing water as it ran across a sandpit directly toward the hunters, who quickly ended its pain with another shot. Perhaps five animals brought down with four rifles. Another fire. More tea. More ribs. This was the time that Gabe brought the ribs to me. It was also the time when he butchered an animal himself.

It's a word now debased, but at the time I confess I saw a kind of nobility in the last struggle of that great dying beautiful animal, one leg dangling, the flash of splashing water in the sunlight, the moments of suspended time, time hanging like pain, drops of water held in the air, the almost endless void of space between each heartbeat of pulsing agony, enough time to think of Catiline's soldiers dying to the last man with all wounds in front, as Sallust tells the tale, time that drips like thick red blood, time that hangs on the shreds of skin and cartilage and bone of a shattered appendage, time that, finally and abruptly and for all eternity, stops. Later I would savour eating the meat. The hunters, ever pragmatic, would quickly determine whose shot had missed and carefully use up a measure of moments in resighting the rifle.

I have been on caribou hunts with Dene in mid-winter, on snow-mobiles east of Fort Good Hope. I have hunted caribou with Inuit on Baffin Island in May on snowmobiles and in August on foot and from boats. I've held the rifle in my hands at times, when invited, and fired the shots. I've carried the meat down mountains or loaded it into sleds or boats. I've done my somewhat pathetic best to help with the skinning, with the butchering. I've savoured fresh tongue, fresh heart, fresh ribs, fresh liver, raw liver (even with dip: don't ask!) in the company of hunters. These stories that I've told, here and now, this is what it was like to hunt caribou with Begade Shutagot'ine on their home ground at Caribou Flats in August 1997.

The Bush Posts

Within a few days I had grown so focused on hunting that other purposes of the trip had trickled from my consciousness. I came to realize that we weren't just hunting to feed ourselves on this trip. The camp was slowly being outfitted with thin spruce-pole frames. The meat was being carefully sliced into thin, flat pieces and hung on the frames. We were there to make dry-meat, as much as we could, which would be shared around the community and would last through freeze-up when caribou hunting could begin again. That was why the hunters weren't satisfied with the two caribou they got at the river. That was why the aim was to get as many as possible at the creek bed. That was why our daily rhythm involved a lazy morning in which I could make journal entries, study the Slavey language (which I never learned), or even read, and an afternoon boat trip in search of more game. In the very dry subarctic air the hanging caribou meat did not rot, it slowly dried. The product, thin slabs of jerky-like meat, are a great Dene delicacy and store well for long periods of time. Begade Shutagot'ine are among the important providers of dry-meat, and Caribou Flats was a prime source. Our trip was a working trip, a hunting trip.

The hunts had drama. They were engrossing affairs, and it was easy to be caught up in the moment. It was the simplest path to become focused or even obsessive, constantly on the lookout for movement or sign of moose caribou sheep. Every boat ride was a hunting trip rich with the possibility of another story. Any empty-handed return seemed slightly tinged with failure, even when we already had meat enough.

So when the boat turned up some small dead-end channel so that David could "show me something," I was barely paying attention, convinced we were checking out another possible caribou ground. We stopped, got out, looked around. There was some talk with Gabe. No sign of caribou. We got back in the boat, went a bit further. We were looking for something. We stopped again. Landed again. Got out of the boat. Looked around. This place seemed more familiar to Gabe, seemed right. Someone called and we all gathered. There it was.

Fixed firmly to the ground near the bank of a side channel of the Begade, about a metre and a half high, a square, point-tipped greying old post: a prospector's or surveyor's post with a brass plaque dulled by time and fixed by screws and folded around near the top, placidly waiting to have its story told.

Suddenly we were back in time: it was 1921 and a chief named Albert Wright had decided that he would leave nothing to chance. In order to ensure that the land of his people continued to be the land of his people, he marked it the way newcomers marked the land, with posts. He filed paperwork and he planted posts deep into the ground, or fixed the metal plaques to tree stumps he cut for the purpose. Some of them are still there.

Suddenly in 1997 I found myself standing in the presence of Chief Albert Wright's work, part of his legacy, part of the heritage of Begade Shutagot'ine: an unmarked marker. There was not much to say. There was not much to do. What little there was, we said and did. I, of course, in my role as documentarian, as recorder, as witness, as secretary, took pictures.

The sight of these silent sentinels brought me back to my own purpose; meat was a by-product of this trip for me. I was here because of a new treaty that purported to extinguish Begade Shutagot'ine title to this land. The elders with whom I worked insisted that if I was to help them, it was necessary for me to have some experience of their land. If I was to understand what this issue was about, I needed to see with my own eyes the places they talked about. If I was to know anything about Begade Shutagot'ine, I would need to be with them on their home territory. Certain things that gave them a sense of the inalienable right of Begade Shutagot'ine to their traditional territory were to be witnessed. These included certain places, certain mountains, certain sacred sites, certain repeated activities, and certain historical traces: these were the "certains" I would hold against the state's insistence upon "certainty." This post was one of the things I was certainly there to witness, to document, to fold into the story.

Chief Albert Wright had put up posts. According to Gabe, with the help of Norman Simmons, at least one of these had been marked in the '70s or '80s with a historical plaque to indicate its significance as a heritage site. The marker was marked with a marker. That one was not the post I saw, nor did I ever see the one with the historical plaque. I did see and document a physical reminder of the close relationship between Begade Shutagot'ine and the land they had used and occupied for countless years. And I saw a legendary marker on the land.

The physical reminder I saw was actually plural in quantity and form: physical reminders, then. The post was one such reminder in one form. Another was the hunting, the camp, the lifestyle, the language, the kindness, the being of Begade Shutagot'ine, all of which testified to the close relationship Begade Shutagot'ine had with their traditional territories. The post, a material object; the hunting, a material practice—both were aspects of the same lesson for me. No doubt things had changed between the way Chief Albert Wright had hunted at Caribou Flats in the 1920s and the way Paul Wright hunted at Caribou Flats in the '90s. But some things had persisted as well.

It was, though, the presence of the post that reminded me that my purpose was not to walk through a culture or a landscape—rich and beautiful and absorbing as these were—but rather to walk through the terrain of history and of politics. The terrain of history and of politics is, as Walter Benjamin well knew, a battle-scarred scorched-earth war zone, where any rules are simply additional tools. The goal of the victors is to erase any memory, any trace of the injustices that were the source of their victory: get the cheerleaders dancing on the ashes of the defeated and send multicoloured balloons into the smoke-strewn skies to insistently celebrate the greatness of the great greedy. Here stood Alexander Mackenzie, here stood Samuel Hearne, here stood Sir John Franklin. Our goals, those of us who walk with humility with the humble, our goals are to puncture those balloons, trip up those cheerleaders, and pull out from the ashes beneath their feet the charred remnants of those charged moments when power exposed itself, when the ancestors confronted their swaggering tormentors. Here stood Edzo. Here stood Akaitcho. Here stood Thanadelthur. Here stood Albert Wright.

The Etchinelle Family

On this trip I became close to the Etchinelle family. David and Theresa eventually hosted me for many of my visits to Tulita, and we travelled with them upriver. James, the oldest of the young men who came along on the trip to Caribou Flats, enjoyed my stories of far-off places, Asia or South America or Europe, that I had visited, and took me along on his hunting excursions. On the surface they were somewhat abrupt and certainly forceful people. Theresa had been chief for a term (1990–91) in Tulita. She was not born to the mountain people but had joined them through her marriage to David. She had strong views and spoke intensely. She was not a domestic type, though in the bush her skills at constructing a spruce bough floor for the canvas wall tent or preparing the caribou meat for drying were exceptional. She worked as hard as any of the men and paid close attention to what was going on around the camp. David was a needler—he liked to find a way to get under people's skins, provoke a reaction from them. He had a big smile, which as often as not held within it some secret, some trick: a knowing smile as much as an enjoying smile. He too was a leader, fully in his element in the bush; he was the camp leader when it came to organizational details and daily rhythms, though he would defer to the elders if they ever expressed an opinion. Mostly, they let him do the hard work of making the decisions and living with the results. He and I had to work closely together as he figured out how much money I really had available to spend and adapted plans to that as much as to the shifting currents and weather and location of game.

Tyler, the youngest, was about eight or ten years old at the time. He watched and learned; one could sense his yearning to join in the work of the hunters. Meanwhile, with his twenty-two (the smallest and most common rifle used) he became the fearsome enemy of ground squirrels. He loved being outdoors, being at the camp, spending time on the river, or playing or doing target practice. While David watched me carefully, smiling, trying to figure me out, seeing what my limits were, James and I would talk. I was impressed with his quiet work ethic, his skills as a hunter and boat driver, his self-possessed self-sufficiency. We shared stories. He wanted to know about Cuba, or New York, or Amsterdam, or Mexico, or Baffin Island, or wherever I recalled my wanderings had taken me. He told me about spring hunts at Drum Lake and the training courses he had been on. We planned a winter hunting trip into the mountains by snowmobile, which I have yet to take.

David Jr. was between Tyler and James, too old to play much, too young to relate well to someone of my age. He was a part of the hunters, though his father kept him close and was still teaching him.

After days of travel and camp life, I added to the partial picture I had formed of the Etchinelle family while in Tulita. They were trying to get by, steady workers at the wage jobs they had found, getting their children set up each one at a time. By the time we left Caribou Flats I knew them as a family of great warmth, strong loyalty. David and Theresa had instilled strength and honesty and courage and kindness into their children; in a world of distorted values where arrogance and avarice are rewarded and where these are constantly propagated through television and other media, they worked doubly hard to ensure that Begade Shutagot'ine values remained a part of their children's lives. The boys were independent, self-sufficient, and respected the autonomy of other people: they stood firmly on the earth.

The Etchinelle family were Begade Shutagot'ine.

Gabe and the Mountains

One time, I was sitting outside my tent making notes in my journal. The tent itself was new: I had invested in it as a gift to myself for use on Baffin Island with the summer program. It was a brand called a Marmot Sparrow and had quite a few bells and whistles for a tent: strong but lightweight, with various flaps and zippers and pockets. I sat in my ground-level camp chair making notes and out of the corner of my eye saw Gabe's lank, tall form approaching. When he got close he leaned over to take a look at the tent, so I started showing off all the various features. Each new commodity presents itself with the fullness of progress and modernity, replacing an older sense of value choices that define the self with the newer sense of brand names that define the self, and I am as enmeshed in this system as anyone.

So there I am showing a patient elder all these zippers and pockets and the way the fly comes off so I can sleep under the stars, as if I'm a salesman. Gabe appears interested, even across the barrier of language, looking quietly, nodding thoughtfully. When there's no more to show I sit down, expecting him to wander off. He sits down beside me. He sees that I'm writing, making notes. He starts naming each of the mountains across the river from us. I fumble, trying to repeat each name, trying to remember which of the names that I can actually pronounce properly is associated with which of the peaks that I can see. I'm pleased that Gabe is making an effort to communicate directly with me and frustrated that I know so little Slavey. I try to write these names in order, from south to north, counting peaks and counting names, never quite having the two add up. But Gabe continues to sit there, repeats when I ask him to repeat. Has even more names for me when we've run through these enough times. He seems to be grappling with English, digging to find some words. Finally he repeats the name of one of the mountains and points at it as he says: "Worth more than eighty million dollars." Eighty million dollars was the full financial value of the Sahtu Treaty. He names another mountain, points again, and says again: "Worth more than eighty million dollars." He hadn't come to look at my tent. He hadn't come to teach me about place names. He said, "One is worth more than eighty million dollars. They give us eighty million dollars for all." Not one mountain, he was insisting, was worth the whole value of the Sahtu Treaty's financial settlement. Finally, when the light went on, I repeated "Not one of these is worth eighty million dollars" and our eyes sank into each other's. I had learned a little bit of something from him, a little bit of something important, and he knew I had learned it, and across the chasm of age the chasm of language, we understood and shared the fact of our understanding and appreciated the fact of our agreement on this matter.

What is the value of a mountain, anyway? All of these mountains—the few names he had mentioned made it clear that there were many—were worth an incalculable amount. But someone had decided that they all could be bought, could all be sold, for a grand total of $80 million. Out of the blue, on a hot day in mid-afternoon, Gabe had come over to tell me something important and it is burned into my memory. It is about priorities, simple priorities, and values, important values. It is about the way one system must put a number on what is ultimately incalculable, while another system remembers the incalculability and patiently tries to remind those of us who can still listen of that: "Not one of those mountains is worth [so little as] eighty million dollars." So says Gabe Etchinelle. And I believe him.

As Long as the Land Shall Last

Paul and David came to Trent University in Peterborough, Ontario, in the winter of 1998. Paul was part of a series of Northern Chair lectures on Dene Ways (*Dene ke*), which I had organized. David was his interpreter. Paul gave a "keynote" lecture one evening at Peter Robinson College but stayed for a full week, meeting with students and talking in a few of the undergraduate classes. One of those classes was my Native Politics and Communities course, a basic primer on Aboriginal rights and politics that I have given under various names in various places.

I invited Paul to talk about whatever he felt was important. He decided to talk about the treaties. I can't remember how he began; perhaps I was too distracted with everyday worries and host worries and administrative worries. But at some point he started talking about the sun, the importance of the sun (*sah* in Slavey), the warmth and the light, the need of living beings for sun. "That was why they made the treaty on the sun," he said ("as long as the sun goes across the sky"). Then he started talking about the water and the rivers, the necessity of living beings for water, the fish we get from rivers, the thirst water quenches, the fact that even plants need water, even animals. "That was why they made the treaty with the river," he said ("as long as the rivers run"). Then he started talking about the grass. How animals feed on the grass, how the grasses were a part of the land, everywhere, how people could make things from the grass, how the grass represented the land and the land was so important for people. "That was why they made the treaty with the grasses," he said ("as long as the grass grows").

I had heard many learned discussions of treaties. I had heard and read quite a few elders from a variety of First Nations talk about treaties. There are books titled *As Long as the Rivers Run* (James Waldram) and *As Long as the Sun Shines* (edited by Getty and Lussier) and *As Long as This Land Shall Last* (René Fumoleau). The phrases, used commonly during speechmaking as part of the treaty process, had been repeated so often that they had become commonplace. For me they had become an everyday currency, signs that had lost their meaning.

I had never heard anyone talk about those words the way Paul talked about them. He gave those words a new life, filled the signs with new possibilities. Something like this, something extraordinarily different than what the conventional terrain of debate respecting treaty interpretation permits, is what the newly court-sanctioned oral history of the treaties opens for us. We cannot say where or exactly with what substance the oral history that is here and there being documented and here and there being passed on will consist of, but very likely it will involve a surprise, an unforeseen, a gift, and a mark of alterity.

The Trickster

We did have, in our little camp at Caribou Flats, a trickster in our midst. He threw little jibes and pulled little stunts, persistently trying to unsettle us, to see if he could pierce the thin veneer of our placid postmodern we've-seen-it-all-before cool calmness. The less we were inclined to show any emotion, the more he tried to produce some effect in us. Perhaps in some way he was taking our measurements, getting a gauge, figuring out our endurance, our patience, our weakness, our willingness to be doormats, our ability to work. He got away with whatever he could get away with; those who knew this was his way let him get away with very little; those who didn't either learned or suffered the consequences (which were never so dire but no doubt not so pleasant either). His name was David Etchinelle.

One time we went out along the river beside the camp to gather spruce boughs in order to make a floor in the canvas wall tent. Neither I nor Kimberly had done this before, but we offered to help and followed David into the bush. He started cutting and piling spruce boughs and made quite a large pile. Then he bundled it up and told me offhandedly to take it back to camp. A few spruce boughs seemed like a light enough load, but this was a rather large pile. When I tested it I realized it was going to be quite heavy. I put it on my shoulder and started to make my way back to camp, cursing under my breath—"Damn, this is heavy"—but assuming we'd all get a load of this nature. When I got out of sight I tried to shift the load and it dropped to the ground, so I half carried and half dragged it back to camp. It was hot in the mid-afternoon sun, I was sweating, the fresh-cut spruce was sticky. I was thinking, with a curse, "These Dene are way too much for me." I was not far from the tent when, looking back, I could see James and Kimberly together carrying a load that was a bit smaller than the one I had. "That so-and-so," I said to myself, "he pulled one over on me!" but I took some pride in having gotten the load back all the way by myself.

I deliberately acted casual, didn't meet his eye when he got back, himself with a smaller and shared load: no big deal, he wanted me to take that load and I had done so. He said something in Slavey to James, who nodded affirmatively; I assume he asked if I had gotten the load all the way back by the way he was looking at me as he posed the question. Now he knew something about me: I was a stubborn so-and-so, and if he gave me too much work to do I'd do it if it killed me. He was careful not to kill me.

Many of the trickster images we get in literary theory seem a bit whitewashed: doing good, a bit clownish, always funny in a lighthearted way. But the trickster bites when your patience is already used up, when you need a moment of quiet, when you don't have the energy to deal with her. The bites can cut and can even be unkind. These aspects of Indigenous culture don't often cross the threshold of idealization that circulates in the dominant culture.

I am very fond of David and I believe he reciprocates my affection. He became the elder and leader I would work with. He too was witnessing what Paul and Gabe were going through in those years, he too was dragged along by them for the ride, and he knew better than most and appreciated what I was trying to contribute. I believe he also knew that I understood and valued what he was trying to contribute. But in our little camp at Caribou Flats, I learned to always be a little wary of him: if my guard went down he would snatch the opportunity and plant something bothersome under my skin. He can't help it, it's in his nature: he's a trickster. Paradoxically, I like him for that, too.

Gabe Butchers a Caribou

One time when we had hunted quite a few caribou, each of the hunters had skinned and butchered one, but a last animal was left. Gabe had started a fire and cooked some meat, and we had tea on. So as each hunter finished butchering, he came to the fire and sat down with some ribs and tea, eating and resting. Gabe went over to the last animal and started to skin it and cut up the meat. Something he did caught James's attention and he got up and went over to watch. So did David. And David Jr.; before long all the Dene were standing in a circle around Gabe as he quickly butchered the caribou.

When I asked what was up, they said he was doing things, using shortcuts, working faster than they had ever seen. These Dene men had been butchering all of their lives, so much so that the fact that it is a skill rarely noted. But Gabe had something to teach them about this daily-bread-like task, and taught simply by doing. It was a caribou-butchering clinic and all the students came away bright-eyed with excitement: they had learned some things about something they did almost every day and were eager to try them. Not a word was said, save by me asking questions afterwards, as always.

I'm not sure that Gabe intended to teach what was learned that day. It is clear that one thing he did want to do was gather some caribou blood in a bag made out of stomach lining, to be boiled and eaten back at camp. Paul was excited about this, as they hadn't had a chance to try fresh boiled caribou blood in years. I said that I would try it too. That summer in Pangnirtung at a community feast they had offered aged walrus and I hadn't had the nerve to try it, but then regretted not doing so since the chance came so rarely. Things like caribou tongue and fish heads had once not been exciting to me, though now I treat them as the delicacies they are. So when we got back to camp and they boiled the blood, eating it with a bit of oatmeal to soak it up, I tried a plate and then had seconds. David was watching me and mentioned that "only the elders feel the need to eat that kind of food" these days. Only Paul, Gabe, and I ate some. It wasn't so bad, though to be honest I can't say that to my taste it was particularly good, either!

Speech and Environmental Ethics

The trip to Caribou Flats was funded in part by the Social Sciences and Humanities Research Council of Canada, which in the mid-1990s had invited applications for what they called a "strategic grant" on the issue of ethics. The proposal that I prepared, based on what my early conversations with Paul had produced, was called "talking about the land: speech and environmental ethics among Begade Shutagot'ine." I was interested in the intersections between two kinds of ethics. The ethics of speech, of speaking, of distinguishing between formal speech, storytelling of various kinds, and casual conversation were of interest, sparked in part by my study of Julie Cruikshank's magisterial work on oral narratives, especially in her *Life Lived Like a Story* and *The Social Life of Stories*, but also sparked by an interest in the social theorist Jürgen Habermas's emphasis on the communicative dimensions of public discourse in books like *Communication and the Evolution of Society*.

In *Life Lived Like a Story*, Cruikshank's complex interwoven narratives were produced through her collaborations with three Dene women from the Yukon (admittedly, "Dene" is a gross over-simplification of their Tlingit/Tagish cultural identifications): Angela Sidney, Kitty Smith, and Annie Ned. It was the kind of book I would love to be able to write, interweaving life narratives, historical narratives, and mythical narratives, while—most difficult of all—managing to translate the "grain of the voices" of these women onto the written page. There are points in this text when you can "hear" the women tell their stories. The text communicates the complex storytelling praxis of these women and enriches our knowledge of the culture of Indigenous Yukoners, exploding the common Pierre Berton banalities of Yukon history and allowing us to learn about the actual lives of actual individual people, an example of the promise of oral narrative. Cruikshank's introductory and concluding essays are remarkable in their own right, as are the collected essays in her follow-up book, *The Social Life of Stories*, though the narratives stand out for their sublime elegance.

Habermas, while somewhat unfortunately tied to an evolutionary narrative of social forms, draws attention to public discourse as a critical feature of contemporary social life. The politics of speech becomes an abiding concern for those familiar with Habermas's paradigm, which nevertheless is grounded within a Marxist framework and thereby avoids the potential of capture within a liberal politics (something that Michel Foucault's sometimes-overlapping work seems to often fall prey to). Habermas studies the "communicative competence" of speech agents and the forums of speech in which different levels of such competence circulates, searching for undistorted forms of communicative practice and universal levels of disinterested speech.

Alongside these texts and issues, and in some form of complex intersection with them, I wanted to study environmental ethics, the appropriate or "good" ways in which Dene interact with the ecological setting that they are connected to. But I was also interested in contemporary modes of Begade Shutagot'ine environmental practice, not some idealized version of the past. How were current policies and frameworks affecting Begade Shutagot'ine life on the land and environmental practices? What obstacles and opportunities, to use current bureaucratic language, were presented under the recent policy frameworks and with the contemporary technologies? This took me straight to the heart of the Sahtu Treaty. At the time of this study I had not read much in the environmental studies field; most of what I looked at had been anthropologically informed work, including Hugh Brody's (2000) and George Wenzel's works on hunting cultures, Robin Riddington's work on Dene culture, Michael Asch's (1993) work on Dene politics: scholarship of the sort that always involved some reflection on the connection between people and land. However, as I reflect and write this text I do so in the shadow of Fikret Berkes's *Sacred Ecology*, which makes a strong argument in favour of using Aboriginal traditional knowledge in land-use planning, and in relation to Paul Nadasdy's *Hunters and Bureaucrats*, which deals with the political difficulties of such arrangements, as well as engaging with broader work by an emerging generation of Indigenous scholars and activists pertaining to environmental issues, such as the work of Glen Coulthard or Audra Simpson.

The "speech and environmental ethics" of my research proposal might have been better translated as environmental speech ethics, though there were elements of each that did not intersect and I was interested in these as well. The time at Caribou Flats gave me an extraordinary opportunity to probe these issues. From Paul I was learning about what he called "good stories" and "strong words," two phrases he often used and to which I paid attention. Every day we were immersed in the land and able to observe and be a part of Begade Shutagot'ine land-based praxis. There were also the powerful moments when the space or time in which these two ethical structures intersected, as when Gabe had said that "not one of these mountains is worth [so little as] eighty million dollars." Speech and environmental ethics right there, folded over each other as they were in the continuing struggle of Begade Shutagot'ine for the continuance of their land rights.

Soon after I started the study I realized that it might prove as fruitful for me as Cruikshank's work with Angela Sidney had been for her. I wanted to visit Paul every summer, learn enough Slavey to communicate with him on his home terrain, document his life, his stories of Dene history, whatever older Dene stories he knew; somehow properly credit him as the holder of this knowledge. While at Caribou Flats I began to collect Dene terms and memorize and practise the language. My confidence had been built a bit by some initial success in studying Inuktitut that summer; my education had never previously included much in the way of language studies, save for a first-year German language course as an undergraduate. But Slavey is tonal. The word *sah* means sun. The word *sah* means bear. The word *sah* means beaver. In their written form as I've inscribed them here, they all look the same, but in speech and in the local orthography they are different. To hear and recognize these subtle differences as an English language speaker is difficult, compounded by that fact that I'm partly tone deaf, as anyone who has had to suffer through hearing me sing can attest! I wasn't going to get far in Dene (Hugh Brody's [1993] discussion of his own difficulties learning Dene language, in his remarkable *The Other Side of Eden*, which appeared much later, gave me a sense of relief around this issue).

For reasons that will become clear, I did not have the time with Paul that would have been necessary for this work to be mostly in his words, as I had hoped it would be. I did hear some life stories from him. And he told some stories of history. And, I later found, he was a great storehouse of Dene creation stories and what go by the name "traditional legends." It was over almost before it started; this work is constructed the way it is as a "second best" option. Something had to be said about these years, about the Begade Shutagot'ine struggle, so I've made it more of my own story than (in this time of generalized narcissism) I wanted. But I also learned some things from Paul from Gabe about speech and environmental ethics, and perhaps a few of those things have already been shared in this text.

The mouth of the Begade, where it meets the Deh Cho.

Bear Rock, where the Bear River meets the Deh Cho
(Mackenzie River), the site of Tulita.

The Etchinelle family in a jet boat.

Sheep Mountain on the Begade.

Paul Wright in Tulita, 1996.

David Etchinelle.

Theresa Etchinelle making dry-meat near Sheep Mountain.

Hunters at Caribou Flats: not vanishing, 2016.

View of Caribou Flats, 2016.

Gabe and Tyler Etchinelle at a post erected in 1921 by Albert Wright, 1997.

Detail of a post at Caribou Flats.

James and Sean Etchinelle at Caribou Flats, 1997.

Hunting with all-terrain vehicles near Stewart Lake.

Canyon on the Redstone River.

David and James Etchinelle putting up signs along the Begade.

View from Sheep Mountain.

A Sheep Hunt

One time, midway through a lazy morning, David mentioned to me casually that we would be hunting sheep that day. They had spotted some. "Where?" I eagerly asked, knowing that we had been on the lookout for sheep since our arrival. "Up there, on the trail," he replied, gesturing to the mountain behind us with his usual broad smile. It was only then that I made out the thin thread-like line of a sheep trail with, as I could see through my binoculars, several white spots on it. Until now I had never even spotted the trail, which every day the elders and hunters in camp had been keeping watch over.

We travelled as two groups in one boat downriver. The first group, with David, Theresa, and David Jr., was dropped off, and Kimberly, James, and I continued about a mile or so further downriver. We started hiking up; though I offered to help, he carried the rifle all the way and I carried a small pack with gear we'd need. As we climbed up the dry creek bed, up the first wooded slope, up the next ridge, further up, ever up, I remembered a story James had told about some hunters who had slipped a large and heavy pipe wrench into someone's pack so that he inadvertently carried it up a mountain; I could almost hear the laughter when he discovered the trick, everyone watching his face . . .

We finally started to get high enough that we were approaching the trail. We were on a narrow, stony, sparsely treed ridge that went in a vertical direction. James left us on the south side and climbed further up, then whistled as a sign for us to join him, staying on our side. When we reached him, we were in position to see a good portion of the trail made by sheep over years and years of walking the same narrow path along sheer cliffs and steep slopes. The other hunters were working their way to a spot a half mile or so northwards. Since the sheep were between us, they would run sooner or later into the rifles of waiting hunters. Even if the hunters missed, the sheep would turn around and end up in the sights of the other team. The trick was to give enough time so that both teams could be in place, so we waited.

The night before James had showed Kimberly how to use a rifle, and she had had a bit of target practice for the first time in her life. He had asked her if she wanted to hunt something and she answered that yes, she did. So when the sheep appeared he used the bolt action to put a bullet in the chamber and wordlessly handed her the rifle. I could see that it was a moment of ethical crisis for her: she had never killed anything bigger than a mosquito, I guessed. She took the rifle, though, and aimed it. But she was unsteady, the heavy rifle was unbraced, and she found it difficult to sight. James touched her shoulder and we quietly moved down to a spot where she could place the rifle on a log and brace it. The sheep, meanwhile, kept placidly meandering closer, almost posing for a perfect shot. "Shoot!" I would whisper under my breath as a perfect opportunity presented itself, but Kim kept waiting. The sheep, though, had no time for my worries. It came closer and closer, presenting side views and front views and more side views: Dene would say it was offering itself. Each time I would think, "Shoot," each time she wouldn't, and then the sheep would come even closer, proving her patience.

It was less than thirty feet away and there was a roar as Kim surprised me, James, herself, and her target by firing. But her shot missed and the sheep turned and started to run down the trail. While I watched, thinking, "I'll never get a chance to hunt a mountain sheep myself!"—ever the self-absorbed intellectual—James had calmly taken the rifle from Kim's hands and ejected the empty bullet casing from the chamber and clicked a new bullet in, quickly passing it to me so that I had the rifle and the sheep was on the last section of the trail we could see and I remembered to brace the barrel with my elbow resting on my chest, with no time to wait or breathe as the sheep rounded the corner out of our sight I managed for a solid second to have it in the rifle sights and squeezed the trigger, for a change doing everything right. Within the roar of the shot the sheep disappeared.

I swore to myself, or perhaps out loud, for having missed. But at least I had had an opportunity and even with the missing I was glad for that. James thought from the sound of the shot, which hadn't gone echoing across the valley, that I actually might have hit the sheep. Either way we weren't too worried; if I had indeed missed, the other hunters would get it. James asked us to stay put and worked his way along the narrow sheep trail to where we had last seen the animal. He came back with the news that it was dead: my shot had struck and it had fallen down a gulch.

We carefully worked our way down to the sheep. I was so excited that I scrambled on the loose rocks the last few feet and cut my leg a bit. James tied the legs of the sheep together and said I needed to drag it downwards on the mountain to a place below, in the trees where the water trickling in the creek at the bottom of the gulch pooled a bit. If we tried to butcher it right there, where it had fallen, he said sheep would never return to that place. He also said it was the Dene way that I should do the carrying and dragging myself; women weren't to touch the animals at this stage. He went back up the trail: there were more sheep to get.

Getting it down to the spot he had indicated was not easy; it was a fairly big animal. I was helped by the fact that we were going downhill, sharply downhill, and following a little creek so I could get water to drink at any spot. No one was around to watch and Kim offered to help, but I felt we should respect the Dene ways, though I sensed she was a bit irritated by this piece of—to her—chauvinism and was the type of person who hated to allow others to do all the work. As we made our way down we heard more shots, three, and guessed that the sheep hunting wasn't over. We reached the spot that it appeared James had indicated, and then waited as we had been told. It was hot, early afternoon by then. After a time James appeared.

Two more sheep had been hunted, he reported, and he got to work skinning and butchering. We watched, I helped a bit pathetically, still not having acquired any of these essential hunting skills.

As he was finished David appeared over the ridge. In a nearby spot he started a fire. The two other sheep, having been killed further along the trail, had been butchered and the other hunters were angling in our direction on their way down, so we all met up and could more easily continue together for the remaining stretch to the boat. I was bursting to spread the word that I had been the hunter for one of these animals, but knowing what I did of Dene ways remembered to hold it in and managed never to say a word about it, either there or when we arrived back at camp. It was a lesson in humility for me that I'm now violating. But to not say anything, to not fill myself up with the story, to know that the others knew what they needed to know, this was a good lesson for me. (It is an unfortunate but deep-rooted family trait that Kulchyskis love to convey any information as soon as they have it, doubly so when it happens to be information that presents them in a favourable light.) While still on the side of the mountain, we got tea boiling and hung sheep ribs over the fire. Then we sat and looked out over the valley, tired and taking our ease, our eyes in the healing presence of a glorious view of land rivers mountains. For the first time since my harrowing trip down the Nahe Deh, I was about to eat Dall sheep meat. And this would be fresh-cooked over an open fire on a mountainside along the Begade with hunting friends.

I also remember and confess that at some point, my calculating mind endlessly calculating—perhaps "trying to find noon at two o'clock," in Baudelaire's words—thinking, August nine, August ten, August eleven, August twelve, August thirteen: it's about two o'clock on a Wednesday afternoon. Already filled with contentment and traces of excitement, I brightened a bit more: "I'm getting paid for this!" I said to myself. It was a cheap joke, but you take your revenge on the system however you can.

After our lunch of the best food in the country in a restaurant with a view one could die happily having seen, it was back to work. The meat was packed, some in canvas packs, some tied together. Everyone had something heavy to carry and it was a long walk down to the boat, albeit downhill albeit with soaring spirits. This is what it is like to hunt sheep in the Mackenzie Mountains with Begade Shutagot'ine.

The boat was loaded and we worked our way back upstream to camp. There we found Gabe, who said just a few quiet words as we were unloading the meat, and James was back in the boat crossing the river to skin and butcher another caribou. Perhaps the greatest hunters are those to whom the game will repeatedly come and offer itself.

I've told this sheep-hunting story in an essay called "hunting stories," but it belongs here too.

Talking about the Land

The time came to leave Caribou Flats. We had done all we came to do seen all we came to see heard all we came to hear. There was more to do and see and hear, but our hourglass had emptied and we had done enough seen enough heard enough. We had only begun to really do something to clearly see something to truly hear some words, to understand a little bit, and while we tried to convince ourselves it was still only noon it was actually two o'clock and it was time to leave. So we left.

Some of us left by prearranged plane, including Kimberly and me. It was important that we take the first plane back so we could help buy another of the perennial and much-needed forty-five-gallon barrel drums of gas for the jet boats, getting it on to the return flight. The plane, though, didn't show up for about five or six hours after the prearranged time. So we sat around at the gravel-strip bit of clearing that served as the Caribou Flats international airport and did what everyone at an international airport does—we waited. The food court at Caribou Flats international airport consisted of this huge blueberry patch. We waited in it. I picked a Styrofoam cup full of berries and took them over to a surprised Gabe, who seemed happy to have them without the work. We waited some more. I picked and ate enough berries for myself that day that my skin probably started to turn blue. We waited even longer. I went for a swim with the boys in a small off-shoot stream of the Begade. The water was pretty cold. After swimming, though, I was able to wait some more.

Gabe started talking to Leon, showed him a spot near a tree. Later Leon walked over to me and took me to the place. It was the place where the bear gets its power from the tree. Leon, a big man, did a good imitation of a bear walking and scratching at the tree, something it does every year before going for its long winter sleep. There were indentations in the ground, not footprints but indentations that had been walked in numerous times, as evidence of the bears' regular presence. "There are more things on heaven and earth than you or I ever dreamed of in our philosophies," said the sage. It gave us something to think about. As we waited. Maybe we're still there. Maybe other beings could get power from that place from those trees.

Bush elders, the elders who have spent a good part of their lives in the bush on the land, hunting and sewing, always have more to say about the land. On any part of the bush in their home territories, they will have stories and place names and see things that the rest of us overlook. Stories fold over onto other stories. The very shape of the land acts as a mnemonic device, calling forth a stream of stories. Gabe and Paul never tired of taking advantage of their appreciative audience and we never tired of taking advantage of them.

Mostly, they talked about the land.

DEPOSITION THREE
Drum Lake

The relationship that First Nations have to land is much broader than rights associated with the ownership of land. The relationship to land is spiritual and sacred. The relationship to land reaches beyond and behind individual ownership, recognizing both past generations (the bones of my ancestors in the land) and future generations (which we refer to as "the faces in the sand"). Earth is mother. Land is seen as part of the "human family."

—PATRICIA MONTURE-ANGUS

There is a "special bond" between Aboriginal peoples and the lands they have traditionally occupied. These bonds should be reflected in the discourses of Aboriginal citizenship. To speak only of Aboriginal control of Aboriginal affairs would disenfranchise most Aboriginal peoples from their traditional lands. Measured separatism would separate many from places they hold dear. Why should an artificial line drawn around my reservation bar me from a relationship with the vast areas my ancestors revered? The marking of such boundaries could prevent the acknowledgement and strengthening of continued Aboriginal reliance, participation, and citizenship with the lands they use outside the lines.

—JOHN BORROWS

Drum Lake

There was more to see, much more to see, of the Begade Shutagot'ine territories, of course. I had only really scratched the surface, had the slightest taste of the lands we were talking about. There were all kinds of places with names that had become talismanic for me: Stewart Lake, Sheep Mountain, Red Dog Mountain, Drum Lake. The last of these, the site of Paul Wright's camp, had become almost mythic to me. Drum Lake was talked about constantly by Begade Shutagot'ine. Stories of travelling there by snowmobile for spring hunts, or of meetings that had been held there by Dene leadership or by the territorial government leaders, or of family events: these were all common choruses for our conversations where the name "Drum Lake" punctuated many a story in the rhythm of its namesake. A photograph of Drum Lake graces the cover of the book *Denendeh: A Dene Celebration.* No doubt taken by René Fumoleau, the photo shows a younger Paul Wright running an outboard motor with a young boy at his side. It was one of the places that Paul and Gabe had said they would take me to, that I had to see, and the desire they instilled had only grown after the trip to Caribou Flats. In August of 1998 I arranged for a chartered plane to take a group of us there. This time, the group included—as well as Paul and me—Krista Pilz, my then partner; Jim Welch, a research assistant who had, as with Kimberly the summer before, proved his value to me on Baffin Island earlier that summer; and Paul's daughter Judith Wright, her husband Fabien Bird, and their two young boys, Joe and Glen. This trip there would be no journey time to get acquainted but rather a mere day or two in Tulita before the flight of slightly more than an hour to Paul's camp at Drum Lake. I was told that the camp was well outfitted, and that we would all be quite comfortable. By then I had learned to entirely trust my Dene hosts, to give myself over to their hospitality.

The flight to Drum Lake was an event in itself, as glorious as the return trip by air from Caribou Flats had been, though on that day I had been so sad to leave, wishing with every breath I was back down below on the river, returning by boat. In such a mood the glory of the mountains seen from a small bush plane lacerated my heart as a too-final reminder of what was being left behind. On the trip to Drum Lake I was filled with the joyous anticipation of arrival, hungrily eager for the days that were to come. We flew from the rolling rounded hills of the Deh Cho into the jagged edges of the Begade mountains with an eagle's-eye view of winding rivers and creeks and sheep slopes and the glory of bush river mountain country. It was not a long trip, perhaps an hour, and then the float plane was circling and landing on a large lake, pulling up to a spot where there were some buildings and a small creek emptied into the lake. There was gear to unload and sort, but Judith and her family were already there and had opened and aired out and cleaned and prepared. The kids were swimming by the time we arrived. Landings happened so fast and suddenly we were out of the plane on a hot dry afternoon walking around Paul's camp at Drum Lake.

The camp was quite an affair, obviously used both by hunters and their families, and by visitors and tourists. There was a main building with quite a large enamel stove, a big room for dining, and several small bedrooms. Then there were about three smaller cabins with bunkbeds for guests. Each had a gas lamp, a desk, a basin and jug for washing, a few chairs, and a few other amenities. There was an outhouse toward the back of camp, as well as a few toolsheds and a teepee for drying meat. The camp was outfitted with a few boats as well, one with a ten-horsepower motor and the others with smaller, three-and-a-half-horsepower "kickers." There was a diesel generator that could be fired up any time we needed electricity. The whole place was set on a spit of sparsely bush-covered land that poked out into the lake, with the lake running along one side and the creek running along the other.

The lake itself curved in a U shape around a long low mountain that lay across the waters in front of the camp. The good fishing was mostly on the other side of this, so our daily excursions tended to involve going by boat toward the point made by this ridge, then around it toward the larger creeks at the other end of the U.

I had always naively assumed that Drum Lake would be round, shaped like a drum from which it derived its name. I was entirely wrong. Eventually, when I asked, I was told that in the spring when the lake from the other side was being struck with something flat, like a beaver tail, it made a noise like the sound of a drum.

The camp and time at Drum Lake didn't have the same dramatic intensity that shot its sparks at Caribou Flats; the time at Drum Lake was more peaceful calm quiet. Slow mornings with time to read or write or go out fishing. Hot afternoons in which we could go out hunting or work at camp or swim or continue the work of reading and writing. It was comfortable from the start; we ate well, especially on the fish and meat we procured. The big advantage of Drum Lake emerged in the graceful space of the evenings, when lit by the warm flickering of gas lamps, screened away from mosquitoes and other annoyances, we could sit quietly in comfortable lounging chairs and let time glide by, riding the currents of Paul's stories. We had come to Drum Lake, first and foremost, to listen.

A Lesson in Listening

Who listens anymore? Certainly not I: my PhD is a licence to speak and I deploy the licence constantly, to the great discomfort of all who encounter me. Given my propensities as a Kulchyski, someone who will talk about anything at great length when afforded the slightest opening, the world would have done well to deny me this licence, but it was unprepared and I slipped beneath the gaze of the guardians, earning a ticket to talk. Actually, the Italian poet-philosopher Giacomo Leopardi diagnosed this symptom of modern times in the nineteenth century: his witty *Pensieri* (Thoughts) make repeated reference to the malaise, the evil of his time, embodied in the fact that everyone wants to speak, wants to dragoon poor innocents into the position of audience. Walter Benjamin was no doubt inspired by Leopardi to some extent in his more well-known essay on the storyteller, in which he comments on the loss of stories as being connected to the loss of boredom, "the dream bird that hatches the egg of experience," without which stories do not take hold. In this tradition now stands Giorgio Agamben who, following Benjamin, has speculated philosophically on the implications of "the destruction of experience."

I had always wanted to talk, to really talk, with Paul. We always seemed to misfire. Certainly he told me a great deal. I was learning from him every day that we spent together, and recorded many rich conversations with him. But we never had one of those conversations that reach into the existential heart of things, I never felt we were fully engaged; of course there were the wide differences of age of culture of language of background, and these things were canyons that were difficult to cross. Yet it felt like he was holding back in some way that I couldn't put my finger on. Until we got to Drum Lake. Until he gently explained to me how I held him back.

One night early on we were settling down in the sitting room, letting the late evening light filter out the daily bothers, preparing to talk. I put my recorder in the space between us. Paul had said he wanted to tell me some stories. It was clear these would not be videos of planes landing and taking off. He said he wanted me to learn to listen in "the Dene way." That meant "no recorder." He would tell me the story and I would have to really listen, listen to learn it. He would repeat the story, and in the repetitions and my attention,

I would capture the story in memory, not on tape. By doing this I would be participating in the Dene oral tradition, not engaging in some vampire-like feeding on a story I hadn't bothered to learn. All that was said at Drum Lake was said off tape, off any record save that of memory itself. It was in memory Dene put their trust, not in machines.

I was taken aback by this request, which I instantly complied with. I had so desperately wanted to "document" Paul's stories, and to do so with the rigid uncompromising accuracy of the best possible recording technologies. In my researcher-centred world view, this was the most respectful thing I could do. I had never reflected on how this set up a barrier between us. It was a strong lesson in pedagogy in research in listening: learn to listen really well. To study the oral tradition, one has to immerse oneself in it, one has to learn the protocols of speech and hearing, one has to exercise one's facility for remembrance. Or perhaps I can articulate it as follows: the best way to preserve the oral tradition is not to fix it on recordings or documents but rather to immerse it in the indefinite space of memory, to pass it on orally, to keep the oral tradition alive rather than place it in another cultural butterfly collection.

When I had been boiled in the cauldron of this simple powerful lesson, we were ready to really talk. Which meant I was starting to be ready to really listen. Which meant Paul began to tell Begade Shutagot'ine creation stories.

Judith Wright

Judith is a force in her own right. She was in many respects our camp leader, occupying the position that David held at Caribou Flats. She organized the financial end of things, working around the limits. Although she didn't go hunting, and although there were fewer daily decisions to make at Drum Lake than at Caribou Flats, whatever was decided—if we would go for a picnic out on the lake that day, or pick berries, or try to bring in more caribou more fish more moose— came down to Judith. Again, she would never go against any express desire on Paul's part, but as often as not he was happy to leave things to her care. So though she ran the kitchen and engaged in what some would call "women's work," she was also in my eyes the camp leader. The kitchen, in fact, is a good position from which to run a hunting camp.

She was the adopted daughter of Paul and Mary Rose, and at that time was living on the Dene reserve at Hay River. Judith is observant and has a lightning-quick mind; there's little that escapes her notice. She has some of Paul's diplomatic skills but as a younger person in the prime of life also has something of a more forceful persona (not that Paul was not forceful in his old age, but in his unfailing politeness and modesty you had to understand a little bit to see it, whereas with Judith it was right there!). At Drum Lake she was agonizing over whether she should give up her work at Hay River and move back to Tulita to be with her dad, who she knew might not be around much longer. Like all such decisions, involving tearing the boys from their familiar school, trying to find work that might be nearly as rewarding, trying to find and set up a new place, it was gut-wrenching. The calm of Drum Lake was a good place to think these difficult issues through, though; being there with Paul was a healing time for us all.

Judith's partner, Fabien, balanced her in complementary ways. He was easygoing in contrast to her intensity, relaxed in opposition to her energetic alertness. They had built a warm family together; the children were well-loved, confident, energetic, mischievous at times, mostly very well-behaved. One basks in the warmth emanating from the hearth of feelings in such families. But one could also sense the strength there, the fierce protective energy, the drive.

Judith had herself worked on documenting her father's stories and had amassed quite a tape collection. We made plans to work on these, to come back to Drum Lake, to continue with the work and the relations, but events and costs conspired against us and it hasn't happened yet. She has so many strengths: her intelligence, her endurance, her kindness, her bush competence, her office competence, her insight, her intensity, her loyalty.

Judith Wright is Begade Shutagot'ine.

Paul's Marten Hunt

One time Paul told me a story from his youth. It was when he was very young, still in his early teens. He was checking some far-flung part of the family's trapping area, toward Fort Norman. He must have been staying on his own in some small cabin, doing a weekly run of traps. Walking along a trail on snowshoes in the deep bush, he saw something out of the corner of his eye, a movement in the trees. It was a marten. Nervous, excited, he put a shell into the chamber of his little twenty-two-gauge rifle and moved himself into position, waiting. The marten moved: he had a clear shot and took it. He killed it instantly with that one shot. He skinned it very carefully, stretched it out on a wooden rack back at the cabin, and had it on top of the pile of furs he later took to the trading post at Fort Norman.

With the value from that one marten he was able to buy his first high-powered rifle. At that time, such an object meant everything in the world to a young hunter. It was moose. It was caribou. It was sheep. It was independence. It was self-sufficiency. It was both a telling product of his skill and an enormous extension of his abilities. It meant he could make a far greater contribution to his family to his people. It meant there could be no doubting that now he was no longer a boy. Now he had become a man. As he walked back on the long trail home, at some point he caught sight of his father in the distance. His father was on the same trail, far up on a hill, coming down toward him. They saw each other and called to each other. Paul lifted up the rifle high into the air held it aloft so from the distance his father could see what he had accomplished. Telling the story years later, he said that even from so far away he could see his "father was so happy, so proud!" It was perhaps one of the happiest moments in his life.

It was a good story. I enjoyed it as he told it. It seemed to make his early life concrete to me, bring some part of him closer.

The two moments of this story, deeply entwined as they are, have distinct significance. In the first instance it is a story of the luck of the hunt, the skill of the hunter in taking advantage of his luck. It is about the way that in the bush, in the middle of nowhere, out of nowhere, comes a life-changing moment. To be ready for that, to be able to take the opportunity, to control the excitement and use the training but still live in that moment: "The surprise that names the instant," writes Derrida (1992b) in his essay on the gift. Hunters experience this gift frequently and must in some sense expect the unexpected, or at least always be prepared for the gift that game will make of itself. Such hunting requires endless measures of patience, the ability to wait, to stoically endure the long walks the long sitting the long lying in the time between times; and then the ability to— *carpe diem!*—seize the moment, in this case, act quickly, make in an instant the right decision, the decisive shot.

The other moment of the story, in which Paul shows his father the rifle, is of another kind of gift entirely. This is the gift of what the best children give back to their parents. The taking flight, raising hearts and spirits, lifting themselves into their own time their own way, becoming themselves. Would that all children could have such a moment. Would that all parents could have such a moment. So many parents, so many children, too many parents, too many children in our sad time are denied even this. This feeling of self-sufficiency of independence, these prized attributes of Dene, this is some part of what it was like to be young and male and Begade Shutagot'ine in the first half of the twentieth century.

For Lake Trout: Fishing Drum Lake

The first thing to be done, to really be done, at Drum Lake was to take a boat tour of the lake, get our bearings, as it were. While doing that, why not catch a few fish? We left in the larger of the boats, Jim, Krista, me, Paul, and Fabien, driving for about ten minutes to the point where the lake curves around the mountain, and then continuing around the bend. Not far on the other side, we stopped at a deep waterhole—Paul knew all the good fishing spots, of course—to try our luck.

Within five minutes Krista had gotten snagged on a log. Or so she thought. She was trying to reel her hook in with some difficulty, so I started to help, pulling the line in hand over hand as she reeled the line. Not far from the boat we realized that it wasn't a log at all, it was a lake trout. A big one. It didn't fight, it too was ready to give itself up to us. We used a net to get it into the boat. Neither Krista nor I had ever seen a fish that size caught with rod and reel. We were both a bit stunned or dazed by how quickly this had happened, how momentous this monster-fish was. I mean, they said the fishing here was good, but really, this was ridiculous. At such a rate we'd have enough fish to feed us for two weeks within half an hour!

Fortunately, the outrageous good luck didn't last. We did get a few more fish, but nothing of that size, which proved the second-largest fish of the whole trip. One other monster-sized fish, a bit larger, was caught about a week later.

We weighed Krista's when we got back to camp and it came in at seventeen-odd pounds. It gave us something to talk about, and years later it was still the one that didn't get away.

By the next morning it was eaten, the foundation of a magnificent bush feast: a single fresh-cooked lake trout providing for the whole camp. We would eat fish often, and also caught some that could be turned into dry-fish, using the same principles as held for making dry-meat. Lake trout too is a gourmand's delight, all subtle flavour and vibrant colour, flaking fleshy texture, one of the great gifts of the deepest northern lake waters. As it happens, one of the attractions of Drum Lake for Dene was its depth, unrecorded, they told us, because it was unmeasurable. But in its deeps it held many treasures to be prized and savoured.

Any time we were at a loss for something to do at Drum Lake, which did happen over the course of two weeks, though relatively rarely, we could always practise the fisher's art, the art of patience, the wait for the sudden surprise of the strike, the rocking of the boat, the lulling of the early or late sun, the sporadic talk competing with the lapping of the waves, the odd sighting of a nearby duck or loon, the lazy cigarettes or songs that float through the drifting thoughts in drift-soaked time, the drifting itself, all the ease of merely drifting drifting drifting . . .

A Grandmother's Grave

Things started to happen fast at Drum Lake, memorable things, powerful things, erupting from the everyday like geysers or volcanoes in moments so packed with meaning that it takes two lifetimes to disentangle them. We would go for a boat ride with Paul, not always entirely sure if the purpose was to hunt or to fish or to go to some place he wanted to see, or to look up into the mountains for sheep, or go off to some other place for a picnic, or perhaps just go for a boat ride.

One time we went out early in the morning on a trip he had been planning and had talked to us about the day before. We were going to look at the old Dene village that had been on the lake, and find his grandmother's grave. There was still mist on the water when we left, the air was brisk especially on the lake, and as we were still half asleep we pulled blankets more tightly around us to keep the warm air pocket that preserved the spell of sleep for a few more moments. We rounded the point and then followed the shore along the other side of the mountains for about twenty minutes. From there we entered the mouth of a river and followed its winding path for another half hour or so. The river was only fifteen or twenty feet across, a small river that wound around tufts of long grasses, reeds, and small waterlogged bushes for about half a kilometre. Once we had stopped here, climbed onto the tufts to look out at a lake beyond, in fruitless search for moose. This time we passed all of the lakes that the river ran by without a thought. Past the reeds and grasses, the river twisted into firmer ground, on which a battalion of spruces stood worshipping the sun, on both sides of the river, densely packed in a throng that reached to the foot of the mountains.

The river twists and turns through this well-treed terrain, with the banks on each side about five or six feet or so above the surface of the water: just high enough that you can't see over to the other side. As often as not, if you climbed up you'd find a view of some other part of the same river and be tempted just to portage over, never quite knowing how long it would take by following the river itself. Here too, as well as the cackles of crows and the guttural geese honking, you might hear the low hoot of a whitish owl with black markings, perched on one of the taller trees partway up a mountain.

At some point, not too far into the bush, we landed the boat and got out. Here the spruce were somewhat sparser. A few old, broken-down cabins, now mostly rotted back into the earth, were the only traces of what had once clearly been a lively Dene village. They were long abandoned, long past any hope of recovery, long missed and not forgotten, but yet in what remained of their presence they called up other people's memories: one could feel the sense of a camp well provided for by the fish game berries birds of Drum Lake; one could hear the fathers calling sons, the mothers calling daughters away from the laughter of play for some task or lesson; one could smell the woodsmoke keeping flies from the dry-meat or slipping out of the teepee where hides were being tanned; one could see in the graceful manner in which people carried themselves that sense of self-reliance that sense of independence that pride of carrying one's own and one's family's weight that Dene women and men shared. No longer the lingering lifting laughter of children for this place, in its peace and ease. Now unnoticed by so very few: soon to be forgotten as those few themselves completed their time. Paul remembered. Paul came back. He brought us with him, this time.

He took us around, naming the families that had lived in those of the cabins that could still be discerned. The day was getting warmer as the sun slowly stepped over the mountain ridges. We walked further back into the bush, through a clearing, into a stand of spruce, crossing the long grass. Paul said he was searching, not quite sure of where it was: it was some time since he had been here, the bush had changed in small ways. But in a few minutes he led us directly to what he was looking for: a small white cross in the trees.

He sat for a few minutes on a log, had a breather. He wanted to gather a bit of firewood, so I helped with that. He picked some particular plants and cleared away the grave site, tending it as best he could. He lit a small fire beside the grave and offered things to the fire that his grandmother had been fond of: candy, tea, flour, tobacco. There was an old, rusted tin cup near the cross; he found it and placed it gently back in position on the cross next to a rusted bowl that also sat there. He spoke, mostly in Slavey but sometimes in a bit of English, talking to his grandmother as if she were sitting there attentively. Finally, from the canvas bag he carried with him he pulled out his hand drum; he beat the drum and sang a few prayer songs, looking up with the rising smoke toward the sky. There was a gentle spiritual strength to each of these sacred moments sacred movements, which touched us and moved us and humbled us, silent awestruck unworthy witnesses.

He spoke to Krista and me about his grandmother, told us some stories, explained what he was doing in terms of feeding the fire and making offerings. We added small offerings of our own to the fire. He allowed me to take some pictures. When all this was done he sat quietly for a small stretch of time.

Then we wordlessly walked back to the boat. Once on the river we chatted again, cheerfully, and made our way slowly back to camp, where it was time to feed the living.

Not Even the Dead Will Be Safe

Walter Benjamin once wrote, in his famous essay called "Theses on the Philosophy of History," that "not even the dead will be safe from the victors." This is entirely true, experienced more by Indigenous peoples the world over these days than by any other social group. The struggle at Kanesatake was, after all, over a graveyard. A rootless society, consisting entirely of possession-owning individuals who travel to wherever the labour market takes them, is not likely to be overly concerned about the bones of its ancestors. In a secular context, what concern might exist is even further diminished. These old things can be bulldozed. Progress has no time for sentimentality. Societies that have ancient ties to particular plots of land, traditional territories, tend to have concerns that extend from the distant past to the distant future. Unlike contemporary cosmopolitan culture, such societies are capable of constructing meaningful, intergenerational communities; such societies are capable of exhibiting strong loyalties to ancient lineages; such societies mark their bonds to a land for lengthy periods. Whether or not these ties matter to the dominant culture, to "us here" rather than "them there," they continue to move and motivate many peoples, including northern hunting peoples. Extinguishment: this means if oil is found near the mouth of a small river that empties into Drum Lake, some oil company can trample crosses and bowls into the dirt, set up a rig and sometime after coffee break drill pipe right through the ancient heart of Paul Wright's grandmother. After all, the oil matters more, doesn't it?

When the World Was New

When I was ready to listen, Paul was ready to talk. When he was ready to talk, he told stories, old stories, stories such as those told by another Dene elder, George Blondin, in his first book, called *When the World Was New: Stories of the Sahtu Dene*, stories about how the animals once talked and how the order of things was established, creation stories. The long days the fresh air the many activities left me tired in the evenings; in spite of the ease and peace I rarely napped. When the long-sought-after storytelling time came, I would often already be half asleep, or would reach that semi-divine state soon after sinking into a too-comfortable chair. Each night Paul repeated the same story, telling more of it, hoping it would seep into some corner of our memories and stay there. In his day, this was what Dene had instead of TV, Paul said.

He began with a story of how Raven stole the sun from Bear. It seems all the animals were miserable, living in darkness, while Bear hoarded the sun across the lake at his own camp. Raven was given the mission of trying to bring the sun back to where it could be shared by all. He went to visit Bear and offered to tell Bear some stories. Bear eagerly agreed, knowing Raven to be an outstanding storyteller. So Raven began to tell stories, long stories, endless stories. Slowly Bear's eyes began to droop. Slowly Bear's head began to nod, then pop up, then nod again. Slowly Bear's body began to slump. After a time, Raven took a stick and poked the coal-burnt end into Bear to see if Bear would wake. At about this time in the story Paul laughed and said perhaps they should poke me with a stick too: I was in that same droopy state, about to allow my sun to be stolen.

The next night he began with a story of how Raven stole the sun from Bear. It seems all the animals were miserable, living in darkness, while Bear hoarded the sun across the lake at his own camp. Raven was given the mission of trying to bring the sun back to where it could be shared by all. He went to visit Bear and offered to tell Bear some stories. Bear eagerly agreed, knowing Raven to be an outstanding storyteller. So Raven began to tell stories, long stories, endless stories. Slowly Bear's eyes began to droop. Slowly Bear's head began to nod, then pop up, then nod again. Slowly Bear's body began to slump. After a time, Raven took a stick and poked the coal-burnt end into Bear to see if Bear would wake. When Bear never budged, Raven knew it was time. He slipped his beak into Bear's bundle and brought out the sun, quickly flying across the lake to where the other animals awaited. At that time the animals could talk, and they knew that when Bear woke he would be angry. They held a meeting and they decided to go somewhere far away where Bear couldn't find them. They packed into a boat to make the long journey to a land where the daylight would serve them well. Meanwhile, Bear had woken, given a roar when he discovered how he had been tricked, and begun to swim, following the animals in hot pursuit. By the time we reached this point in the story, Paul himself was tired: it was time for sleep, time to try again on the morrow.

The next night he began with a story of how Raven stole the sun from Bear. It seems all the animals were miserable, living in darkness, while Bear hoarded the sun over the lake at his own camp. Raven was given the mission of trying to bring the sun back to where it could be shared by all. He went to visit Bear and offered to tell Bear some stories. Bear eagerly agreed, knowing Raven to be an outstanding storyteller. So Raven began to tell stories, long stories, endless stories. Slowly Bear's eyes began to droop. Slowly Bear's head began to nod, then pop up, then nod again. Slowly Bear's body began to slump. After a time, Raven took a stick and poked the coal-burnt end into Bear to see if Bear would wake. When Bear never budged, Raven knew it was time. He slipped his beak into Bear's bundle and brought out the sun, quickly flying across the lake to where the other animals awaited. At that time the animals could talk, and they knew that when Bear woke he would be angry. They held a meeting and they decided to go somewhere far away where Bear couldn't find them. They packed into a boat to make the long journey to a land where the daylight would serve them well. Meanwhile, Bear had woken, given a roar when he discovered how he had been tricked, and begun to swim, following the animals in hot pursuit. They travelled far, over mountains and over rivers, Bear pursuing them the whole way. Finally they reached a large body of water and, using their boat, went far out into it, attempting to shake Bear off their path. Lost in the water, with no land in sight, they realized they would need to make land of their own. They sent down their best swimmers, Beaver and Weasel, to try and bring up some land from the bottom, but with no luck. Finally Squirrel offered to try; though they doubted his ability to succeed, they let him try. Squirrel dived deep deep deep into the dark waters and was gone for a long time. Eventually his body floated to the surface, clutching a small piece of precious land. From this they made the land, and freed the sun to roam across the sky . . .

These are not Paul's words, they are mine. This is what I remember of the stories he told, precious little: a poor summary in my own words. Better anthropologists than I will recognize some of these stories, earth-diver stories and Raven stories, and probably would have had something far more interesting to say about them than I, a poor choice to be gifted such rich narrative. With Paul, one story blended into another, then another, and another, and on they went. In fact this story didn't end; we never had time to finish it and perhaps there never could be such time. Repeating the story on the page does not duplicate the effect of hearing the story a second time and a third time and a fourth time. Repeating on the page, as I have done here in order to approximate the experience of listening to these stories, is no doubt tedious for the reader who more often than not will skip along until the new part starts. For the listener, each telling is fresh, with new words and asides and humorous interjections thrown in, with enjoyment of the parts one knows and anticipation of the new parts. I waited each time, foolishly, for the finish, finally on about the fifth night realizing that such closure was beside the point: we were well into another "new" story or chapter or stage. Why make a boundary between one story and the next? Paul had no need for such definition, and his stories taught me that perhaps I had no such need as well.

A credible, important, French contemporary philosopher of the post-structuralist school, Jean-Luc Nancy, sets a scene in his study *The Inoperative Community* of listeners gathered around a campfire to hear the story. For Nancy, such a scene has disappeared. But he makes a great deal out of the fact that such stories are critical to the constitution of community, to a form of community that deserves to be called such and not the debased alienated collectives often self-proclaiming such status ("the University of Manitoba community," the "business community," and so on; as if such near completely serialized individual collectives can recover a bond they exist to destroy, by proclaiming in their moment of destruction that they have achieved it). Nancy's insight into the loss of community among contemporary collectives is philosophically compelling. His sense that all such communities have disappeared, that such stories are no longer told, is Eurocentric hubris: a projection onto other parts of the world of that which is endemic to dominant, Western, modernist, capitalist social collectives. An earlier French philosopher whose reputation has waned in recent decades, Jean-Paul Sartre, offered more fruitful advice by carefully distinguishing between alienated (serial) collectives and forms of community (the fused group) where mutuality in a meaningful sense still prevails. Nancy's essay does contain another insight, which is that such creation stories are constitutive of meaningful community: this community tells this story of its own origin of the world's origin; this story is this community, this community is this story.

If Nancy is correct, in listening to and learning Paul's Begade Shutagot'ine creation story/ies, in those precious ephemeral moments, we were part of reconstituting Begade Shutagot'ine. Not, I must insist, that I or we "became" Begade Shutagot'ine but rather that we stood with Begade Shutagot'ine in the charmed circle of their storied self-creation.

These stories were Begade Shutagot'ine.

On Boundaries

In a way, just as I had wanted to frame Paul's stories with beginnings and endings, creating my own sense of definitions, so too the impulse to establish boundaries operates through the state. The extinguishment policy is one direct result of such an impulse.

The extinguishment policy underwrites at least three critical boundaries that will play a continuing role in the lives of Begade Shutagot'ine. The first of these is the boundary between Crown lands and Sahtu lands. Sahtu Dene and Metis now have two forms of title over two forms of land. On the one hand, they have title to a small portion of land that includes subsurface rights: the rights to own any mineral or energy resources that can be found on or under this land. On the other hand, they have only surface title or rights to a larger portion of land. Together, these two categories of land amount to about one-tenth of the whole Sahtu region. The other 90 percent of the land in the Sahtu is purportedly owned by the Crown, which has exclusive jurisdiction save where it has transferred such jurisdiction or ownership to a third party (a homeowner or an oil company, to take two common albeit disparate examples). These categories of land are very clearly and precisely surveyed and marked on maps or, in our digital era, stored in geographic information systems.

The Crown can ultimately do what it likes on Crown lands, though a small percentage of revenue generated from taxation of resource development must be paid to Sahtu Dene and Metis. Sahtu Dene and Metis can ultimately do what they like on Sahtu Dene and Metis subsurface title lands, though something that would have a major environmental impact on Crown lands would doubtless need Crown approval. On those lands to which Dene and Metis have only surface rights, a complicated set of procedures is invoked if a private company decides with Crown support to develop a resource: compensation, which might include added equivalent amounts to the Dene and Metis surface rights land quantum, must be negotiated. The Sahtu Treaty establishes a series of land and water and environmental impact joint management boards, reporting to the appropriate federal minister and Dene and Metis Sahtu bodies. In my view, "sharing the land" in the manner envisaged by Paul would have amounted to having the whole Sahtu region classified in the manner of the surface rights regime, though with Aboriginal title unsurrendered. Such a move would have involved less boundary making, but no doubt more uncertainty.

A second boundary established through the Sahtu Treaty is between Dene and Metis in one region and those in another. This includes a boundary with the Gwich'in to the north, with the Tlicho (or Dogrib) to the south and east, and with the Dehcho region to the south and west. The last of these was the boundary occupied by Begade Shutagot'ine, who legitimately wanted to join the Dehcho but were prevented from doing so by the whim of federal officials and the complicity of Sahtu Dene and Metis political leaders (the latter were certainly not interested in "pushing" this issue, and at most can be accused of working to "bury" the question: the more people and lands included in the treaty they negotiated, the larger the financial settlement). This also includes a boundary established in earlier years between the Dene and Metis in the Yukon and Dene and Metis in Denendeh. Dene and Metis in all these regions inter-married, traded, gambled, celebrated, allied, warred, and mixed and unmixed with each other. The cultural boundary was far more po-rous than the lines on maps, including the maps of many an anthro-pologist, would have it. These lines these boundaries divide what was once a shifting, organically connected and disconnected nation of peoples.

The Sahtu Treaty also demarcates a third important boundary, that between beneficiaries and non-beneficiaries. This parallels, in some respect, the debilitating and highly charged boundary between status and non-status Indians that exists in the Indian Act. A benefi-ciary is an individual who has signed up as a member of the Sahtu Treaty, is eligible to benefit from its provisions, and has children eligible to benefit from its provisions. A non-beneficiary may be a non-Native person who lives in the region, an Indigenous person who is not Dene or Metis from the Sahtu region (say, a Gwich'in beneficiary, or a Nisga'a person), or a Sahtu Dene or Metis who, for whatever reason, has not signed on as a beneficiary. Say, for example, because they do not want to extinguish their Aboriginal title. Say, for example, many of the Begade Shutagot'ine in the decade of the '90s.

All these forms of boundaries draw lines between people as much as they draw lines on maps and on papers. There are strong currents in contemporary philosophy that challenge this form of boundary drawing. Drucilla Cornell, an important feminist legal philosopher, calls the philosophy of deconstruction a "philosophy of the limit" precisely because of the deconstructive insistence on questioning the viability of such boundaries. The state, as a machine for alien inscription of a certain kind of disembodied writing, must develop and impose such boundaries to achieve its ultimate end: establishing a regime conducive to the accumulation of capital. Such a regime will flourish where certainty of land title and certainty of group affiliation are established. Fluid, organic, qualitative relationships, such as those established among people and between Dene and Metis and their territories, are not conducive to capital accumulation and the totalizing order that dominates contemporary society. This is what Begade Shutagot'ine found themselves, in every fibre of their being, in opposition to in the last few decades. Begade Shutagot'ine wanted to share, wanted some form of politics that did not involve boundaries. But in this world, boundaries are inseparable from politics, which is precisely the determining of which "side" one stands on. Of course, being Begade Shutagot'ine and the notion that others are not Begade Shutagot'ine likewise involves a boundary. But Paul would have happily invited everyone to be Begade Shutagot'ine; that was his way. The struggle against these divisions inscribed by the state was perhaps a hopeless struggle an impossible struggle. It was a great and principled stand. It was not the last such stand. It may yet, in some version of the Sartrean "loser wins," find a way.

What Gets Lost/Poisoned Gifts

One time, Jim and I went up a mountain off the river at the far end of Drum Lake. We started our trip in the coolness of the morning, though by the time we finished it had become another hot dry sleepy afternoon. We landed the boat at a bend in the river and walked confidently inland toward the mountain, circumnavigating a lake in order to get to its foot. Then we walked up and up and up the steep slopes, up and up and up the gravel slides, up and up and up into the sparse trees to the treeless ridge, and up and up and up past the mist the cloud that hung along the mountain, going further on and higher, trying to reach where we might be able to see over and thereby perhaps across some vast distance see sheep. We got another of those delicate treats your feet deliver to your eyes, a view of the lake and the river valley, but our hunting desires were frustrated: no sheep to be seen.

We were happy with our view, though, and happy to sit and have a snack and feel like we had done something that day. Above the mist we were warmed, and by the time we started down the mist had dissipated. In the ease of walking and sliding downwards I almost missed the owl that sat and posed on a scrub pine tree about a third of the way down the mountain, napping perhaps, also lazing away the afternoon in its own way, preparing for its own hunting time. We came to the bottom, and struck out toward the boat. At some point, I forget why, Jim wandered off one way and I the other. The river was right in front of us, one just had to strike out directly away from the mountain to reach it.

In ten minutes or so I did reach it, on my own. But the part of the river I reached had no boat, no Jim. I called out but got no answer. So I started to walk along the river, its current telling me what direction to go. After another ten minutes, or twenty, there was still no boat. No Jim. Had the boat somehow slipped into the river and been taken out to the lake by the current? It seemed impossible, but also seemed impossible that I could have missed it. And where was Jim, anyway? Occasionally it comes back to you that you are, after all, hundreds of miles into what is called "wilderness," relying pretty much entirely on yourself and only a few small mistakes from disaster. I had already experienced a few hundred metres of travel on the Nahe Deh hanging on to an upside-down canoe, so I knew fairly clearly how easy it is for mild everyday enjoyment to quickly turn into terrifying life-and-death struggle. Of course, if we didn't show up back at camp someone would come looking for us. Of course, as long as I stayed along the river they would find me. But how long would it take? When would they come?

It was another ten minutes, or twenty—I had no watch—and I was walking along the twisting and turning bank of the river, and still there was no boat. No Jim. No sign of either. I had a lot of time to think the worst. Which, even with my own paucity of imagination, was an easy assignment. Perhaps I should get used to spending more time alone. Another stretch of time, perhaps ten minutes, perhaps twenty, and I was starting to feel seriously uncomfortable. This was ridiculous. The boat had been right there! How could it have disappeared? Even if it had slipped back into the river somehow, the current was not so strong, the river so crooked—it couldn't have gotten very far. And what the hell could have happened to Jim, anyway? At some point in my walking I realized that I might well have first reached the river beyond where we had parked the boat and was now walking further and further away from it. That, too, was a sobering thought. Should I turn around, walk all the way I had gone, and strike out in the other direction? Could I even find or recognize the point where I had started? Probably not, the whole damn thing looked the same. Inept scholarly types shouldn't be trusted with rifles or left alone in the bush. By now I had gone another ten minutes, or twenty. I called out to Jim again. Still didn't see the boat. It must have been an hour of walking along this damn twisting little river, looking at the next empty bend, trudging along the bank, mind filled with endless little worries, letting them add up to big worries.

Then I rounded a bend and there it was, the boat in all its glory, tied up just where we had left it. The river had so many twists and turns that the slightest miscalculation of my angle of approach meant I had reached a bend, and by following the river instead of striking over land, I had gone quite a long way around. Jim showed up about ten minutes later. I neglected to mention my experience to him, and we carried on as if nothing had happened because, after all, nothing had happened.

On our way back we spotted some caribou near the shore of the lake, almost at the place where Krista had caught her big trout. We pulled in, went after them and actually got one, which Jim butchered on his own, being a practically skilled sort of guy, and so we also brought back meat to camp that day. By the time we got back it was long after my little wandering non-experience, which had receded further into the background: why mention it to anyone at all? The meat we brought made it seem as if I wasn't entirely useless, and really it was only necessary for me to be the one to know the dark truth of my own ineptitude.

Dene prize self-reliance and independence. It is easy to travel on the land with Begade Shutagot'ine and take for granted their many skills. To not take those skills for granted, it is useful to realize how terrifying it can be to truly have to rely entirely on your own in what for Dene is home, but for *mola* is the fearful forest. Even I, who had come to love this land; even I, who have perhaps more bush skills than the average city dweller; even I, who grew up in bush country and have spent as much time as I can with Dene and Inuit hunters; even I know how the thread of my life depends so much on the hunters I travel with. I am, ultimately, at a loss on the land in the bush, or more accurately, lost. I am not self-reliant. I am not independent. Not there. My great friend and sometimes co-author Frank Tester, I must confess, has far more confidence and ability than I. It is a measure or indicator of Begade Shutagot'ine kindness that I was consistently treated with so much respect. It is a matter of little surprise that I would reciprocate it.

The tragedy is that totalizing power works its insidious designs by giving just enough to create dependence, giving just enough to create reliance on others. The favoured mechanism of the last half of the twentieth century through the beginning of the twenty-first century has been the loan and the debt it creates: the loan begets instant dependence, instant reliance, and through the magic of interest compounds and increases the dependence and reliance indefinitely, until forgiving a miniscule portion of the debt seems a great favour. This is the work of the International Monetary Fund, but it is also practised in northern Canada by the state: loan a community funds to negotiate a land claim and thereby ensure they will be forced to sign such a claim as the only way they can pay that debt. The next favoured mechanism is a simple exchange: in exchange for title to land, a small capital stake, just enough to tie a people into the logic of capital accumulation, just enough to create dependence, reliance. For Begade Shutagot'ine the Sahtu claim was a mechanism for eroding their great attributes. What was being extinguished, what was being surrendered were those most-prized elements: independence and self-reliance. The reach of the state, its ability to more easily achieve any of its capricious goals in whatever stage of capital accumulation it is supporting, is dramatically enhanced when it deals with a dependent, reliant people. A dependent, reliant people are a pliable people who will not stand up when the next sacred piece of land is defiled. In my time with them, Begade Shutagot'ine were not such a people. Paul Wright, Gabe Etchinelle knew with a kind of stark clarity that the gifts presented by the state were versions of the gifts of Sinon, poisoned lies, as *The Aeneid* has it.

Hunting at Drum Lake

One time we decided to gather very early in the morning and see if we could bring some fresh meat to camp. We got up earlier than usual, mist still on the water cool morning air piercing our lungs, and with some bannock and tea made our way into a boat and out onto the lake. We rounded again the big bend, making toward the river. Paul and Jim and Fabien were in the front of the boat, I was in the back with Krista not paying much attention. Hunting would begin when we were somewhere up the river, stopping to walk into a lake or stopping at some other spot Paul would know. I had a few moments to gather my thoughts, shift my consciousness from half asleep to half awake, slowly make my way into the day. Suddenly the driver was "gunning" the boat motor, the pitch increasing as the power increased. They had spotted caribou up ahead. Guns were being prepared. I saw some bushes on the flats near the mouth of the river jerk upwards, start to move, shots were being fired, the bushes were antlers, the movement caribou: we got both. I was awake. It was over. The caribou had been in shallow, watery reed flats, not a good place for butchering. We landed on shore and then Fabien and Jim took the boat back, tied a rope, and one at a time the animals were dragged over to shore where they could be skinned and cut up.

Then the long butchering process began. While Paul and Jim and Fabien were working diligently at this, Krista and I wandered around, not even thinking enough to start a fire and get the perpetual pot of tea boiling. A few flies started to buzz around the carcasses as the day began to warm. I was wandering in widening stretches, walking along the shore a bit, each time going a bit further from the activity, when I saw something, some bit of movement. It was a young moose, further along from where the caribou had been. I slowly backed away without making any sudden movements, found Paul rinsing his knife in the lake and gestured toward the animal. He walked calmly back toward the boat where the rifles were, said a few words in Slavey to Fabien, who dropped what he was doing, picked up a rifle, and began to move along the shore for a good shot at the moose. Slowly, person by person, everyone in the group was alerted so we would continue to be quiet and deliberate in our movements. This time, we all watched the shot and we all saw the animal crumple: another set of meals had been added to our stores.

In those moments I felt the wealth of the bush store, the bounty of the land, to use a clichéd comment. I remember once showing photographs I had taken near Yellowknife to my brilliant friend Himani Bannerji, who commented on how "barren" the bush looked to her. I was shocked: this was lush bush, home of rabbits, of moose, of beavers, so much so plentiful. But she, habituated to the agriculturally dense landscape of rural Bengal, found the bush landscape unproductive to her gaze. That was many years earlier. At that time, I hadn't had the experience of hunting when one set of game rapidly follows the hunting of another. From lake trout to caribou from caribou to moose, Drum Lake provided for us, a nurturing and nourishing land where hunting and fishing amounted to going out and getting what one needed, where the animals and fish offered themselves in their part of a complex reciprocal bargain. By doing so, they kept a compact that allowed their brethren to roam free across a vast and beautiful terrain. Paradoxically, those who hunt and kill animals have a much stronger ethical claim in relation to them. Those who confine and systematically factory-slaughter animals have, in my view, no moral sanction, no ethical ground from which to condemn hunters. Though, of course, that won't prevent them from continuing to do so in the harshest and most self-superior tones.

Paul's Medicine Power

A key epistemological and cultural and spiritual fact for many Dene is the existence of what is called medicine power. Medicine power involves the "medicine" one may have with or from some spirit or animal or thing. There is a serendipity to how much medicine power any individual can have: the way one acquires it is as a gift one is born with. One can do some things to enhance one's medicine, but the strongest medicine power comes with birth. Dene rarely talk about medicine power; most of what I know of it comes from George Blondin's books, especially his *Yamoria the Lawmaker*. George's decision to say anything about medicine power was very controversial among Dene elders; one loses one's medicine power by talking about it. George tells a story in the book of how, when he was young, he ran from the grandfather-spirit that was trying to bring him medicine in a dream, and as a result he never gained any. Perhaps he feels he can talk about it since he has none to lose. He fears Dene losing their knowledge of the old ways, and his motivation in talking about medicine power is to ensure younger Dene know a little bit about it.

Many of the old stories, a genre of stories that parallels the genre of stolen women stories that Cruikshank's storytelling elders relate, are stories of war or fights that involve medicine power. These are stories of powerful holders of medicine, who usually look like everyday normal, even poor, people, though they actually hold great power. In the stories, they come in conflict with each other and use their powers against each other. In Dene hand games, where high-stakes gambling frequently takes place, consistent winners are usually thought to have used medicine; the hand games are a practice in which medicine power fights are contained through a socially sanctioned status and wealth war. Blondin constantly insists that medicine should be used for the good of the people, not for self-aggrandizement and not for bad purposes. To know what is going on in many of the Dene stories, though, you need to know about medicine power, so for better or worse George has broken the silence that surrounds the subject.

One of the medicine power stories George liked to tell me during a visit south that I had sponsored as part of the 1998 *Dene ke* (Dene Ways) series was clearly a mountain Dene story. In it, a man had medicine power over stone. One time, he and his people are travelling by boat down a river and the boat gets hung up in the river on some rock. The people are all in danger, trapped, the boat threatening at any moment to tip or flood or tear apart. The people start calling to the man, saying, "You say you have power over stone. Now is the time to use it if you're ever going to." So the man replies, "All right, all right, I'll see what I can do," and calls upon his powers. The rocks get blasted to bits and the boat gets unstuck, so the people can safely continue their voyage. I never did determine why George insisted on telling me this story, but I heard it several times. Perhaps he wanted me to repeat it in my own words here. Perhaps it is because my name is Peter. Perhaps I'll find a better reason some years from now.

One time, Paul and I and his grandsons were sitting at the kitchen table, having just finished lunch. We were idly chatting about nothing in particular, about to get up and go our own ways, when one of the kids said, "Grandpa, you have a lot of medicine power, don't you?" Paul looked over at me, and said, "No, no, I don't have any power. Anyways, you're not supposed to talk about it if you do." His last words were clearly directed at me. His grandson pressed, "No, no, you sure have medicine power, lots of medicine power," and again he replied, "I don't have any," looking at his grandson, and "You're not supposed to say anything if you do," looking at me.

Dialectical materialists such as myself tend not to have much truck with spirits, though part of the power of Michael Taussig's well-regarded work is his insistence on the importance of "re-enchanting" the world, respecting the magic of people and deconstructing the magic of the state. I'm not only a materialist but an atheist and an existentialist as well, as godless a person as there ever was. My friend Bella T'seleie teasingly calls me a "pagan," though in my own world view pagans subscribe to non-Christian beliefs, and I have no such spiritual belief structure. I do agree with Michael Taussig (1994) about the importance of re-enchanting the world. And I think dour Marxists miss the little boat sitting on the shores of the small winding river just a bit by insisting that since "religion is the opium of the people," everyone should attend a re-education camp so they can enter into a secular, despiritualized world view. My criticism of this perspective in some large measure is simply that it is boring.

Working with Indigenous peoples, for whom spirituality is a central tenet, is a challenge for Marxist atheist materialist existentialists. I cheer for immanence over transcendence. But we can untie the knot by analytically distinguishing between religion and spirituality as one of the distinctions that operates along the fault line between the agricultural and capitalist modes of production (religious and religious-secular) on the one hand, and the gathering, fishing and hunting, or bush, mode of production (spiritual-secular) on the other. The latter form of belief is embedded in egalitarian social rituals while the former relentlessly reinscribes hierarchies. Religion in my view involves the institutionalization of spirituality in a codified set of hierarchical social structures; it is a largely patriarchal, largely ideological, alienated, and even despiritualized structure of containment that retains a kernel of its original promise. Spirituality is that original promise, a working through of the mystery of life the magic of the gift the wonder of the world the enchantment of the evening light. Spirituality confronts the questions that many people have needed and likely will continue to need to acknowledge about the meaning of their lives and of life itself. Stanley Diamond has rightly seen in hunting peoples what he calls a "primitive existentialism," which is where the "secular" comes from in my typology above. There must be a form of Marxism that can accommodate this—even while insisting that people create meaning and give their lives meaning, is it not possible to recognize that that spirituality is one of a series of answers to the question? Such an answer satisfies some of us, but will never satisfy all. Should we force everyone to see the "brutal truth" rather than "live in illusion," or should we respect the right of everyone to come to terms in their own manner with the fact of mortality the miracle of birth?

Did Paul have medicine power? Even before his grandson posed the question, I had thought long and hard about the issue. It's clear that he had as well. The way he looked at me was unmistakeable: it was an "I'm not telling" look. I had by then come to the conclusion, which I still subscribe to, that Paul had power over words. He could use words in a way that I've seen no one else deploy them. His words drew me to him in the very first instance. The power of his words, strong words, was what he was known for. His strong words were not angry words, loud words, shouted words, nasty words; they were good, forceful, powerful words, compelling words. Strong words, as Dene say, good stories. If someone could have "weasel power" or power from rocks, or power from stars, or power from caribou, it seemed plausible to me, novice in these matters as I am, that someone could have power from words. If that is possible, then whatever other forms of medicine Paul may have had—and one person could have many forms of medicine if they were particularly fortunate— he certainly had in his personal arsenal power over words.

Culture

What are Begade Shutagot'ine? A people? A race? A nation? A fragment of a nation? Here is where the concept of culture comes into play. The words themselves tell us that Begade Shutagot'ine are a people: Gravel River Mountain Dene/Gravel River Mountain people. The *t'ine* part of the self-designation means people. What is it that makes Begade Shutagot'ine distinct? The name indicates one thing: a location. The people of the Gravel River area of the Mackenzie Mountains. The tie to a specific territory of land is a critical feature in the self-definition of Begade Shutagot'ine. In the language of contemporary social theory, it could be argued that such a tie, or the fact of location, is a necessary part of Begade Shutagot'ine identity but not a sufficient one. In order to live in this part of Denendeh, there are attributes one will have, certain knowledge; one will be the latest incarnation of a certain heritage and history; one will have practised certain activities at certain times of year. These things may be said to be the "ways" (*ke*) of Begade Shutagot'ine, or what could also be called their culture.

The concept of culture, after serving illustrious service as one of the great collective intellectual inventions of the twentieth century, is now in retreat. Social theorists see it as too bounded, in much the same way I have concerns about the many boundaries imposed by the extinguishment clause of the Sahtu Treaty. Certainly there is some slippage in Begade Shutagot'ine identity: Theresa Etchinelle comes from lands to the east of the Deh Cho, for example. Ties of family extend north and south along the Deh Cho. My friend Isidore Manuel from Fort Good Hope is a nephew of Paul Wright; Isidore is a Mountain Dene, though from further north in the mountains. In wanting to join the Dehcho region, Begade Shutagot'ine were choosing where they would like to position themselves, what boundary they wanted to be within and what boundary they wanted to be without. The concern with boundaries, then, must be able to draw distinctions between boundaries imposed from without and boundaries chosen from within. Any group identity, self-naming, will be an inclusive and exclusive process: some will be brought into the circle and some will be defined out of it. There may be more or less movement across the boundary depending upon a variety of factors, and in different contexts the politics of such movement or lack of movement may be oppressive or emancipatory. Each situation demands its own careful interpretations and contextual readings.

Begade Shutagot'ine have a distinct history; they have distinct stories; they have distinct technology; they are distinct families; they have a distinct territory. They are related but distinguishable from their neighbours. They are a very small group of people. In spite of their extraordinary independence of spirit and self-reliance, they do not have self-determination.

Sacred Sites I

What is sacred? Begade Shutagot'ine showed me many different places that they associated with ancient stories and considered sacred sites, where offerings were made and thanks were given. Some of these were part of the key sacred sites of the Dene Nation as a whole. One time, travelling north from Tulita on the Deh Cho, outside of Begade Shutagot'ine territory but still in the Sahtu, David pulled the boat over on the east side of the river, not far from Bear Rock. A small trickle of water, barely visible, seemed to bubble up from the low sloping bank of the river and flow into the Deh Cho. This water was held in reverence, and something was left in order for something (some water) to be taken.

What is sacred? Bear Rock itself, the mountain that overlooks Tulita as part of the everyday landscape, is the sacred site represented in the logo of the Dene Nation. It was on Bear Rock that Yamoria the Lawmaker pinned the hides of the giant beavers he had chased around and out of Sahtu (Great Bear Lake), down the Sahtu Deh (Great Bear River) to the Deh Cho, where he killed them with his giant arrows. On the south face of Bear Rock are clearings in the treed slope in the shape of skinned beaver hides. This event, the killing of the giant beavers, was a critical point in Dene history when Yamoria started establishing laws for the world: giant carnivorous or otherwise troublesome animals would no longer be able to terrorize the people. To this day you can see the reminder of Yamoria's great work, inscribed on the face of a mountain.

What is sacred? Travelling up the Begade to Caribou Flats, we offer a few bullets to Red Dog Mountain: shots are fired, bullets are also left on a flat rock near the bottom. This takes place as well in the film

The Last Moose-Skin Boat. Only much later would I hear the story of Red Dog Mountain. But I always knew that it is a specifically sacred site to Begade Shutagot'ine, known and reverenced by them.

What is sacred? Stories circulate around these places; ceremonial practices are engaged in at these locations. Is it the stories, the practices, the sites themselves that hold their meaning, that characterize their special status? Or is it all of these things? A Marxist atheist materialist existentialist can only pose questions, is not well positioned to give answers. Though perhaps one can at least note the existence of the sites and the stories the practices and the places when one encounters them.

Sacred Sites *II*

Categorization: when all else fails, one can categorize. This may be one of the lowest forms of thinking or a basic building block of the scientific method, depending upon your preferences. The Teaching Rocks near Curve Lake Anishnaabe First Nation, officially known as the Peterborough Petroglyphs, have been contained and framed by an interpretive centre designed to protect the site. Since the time that the centre was built, the sound of water that once could be heard at the site has disappeared. But traditional spiritual people still have round-the-clock access to the site and the site is generally now in the control of the nearby Curve Lake First Nation, albeit through the institutional structure of a provincial park. The Teaching Rocks are an enormously rich, complex, embodied writing, containing striking single images and a number of repeated themes and images. One can imagine stories told along several overlapping trajectories running in any possible direction, with multiple beginnings and endings and repetitions. One can imagine.

The interpretive signs, though, for the tourists or visitors, are another text altogether. They tell us that this snake-like symbol has been found at x number of sites in northern Ontario; this pelican-like symbol has been found dispersed at y number of sites, and so on. The "explanation" actually tells us nothing, though in a great enough written barrage that there is every appearance of scientific encapsulation. Certainly it wouldn't do to create the impression that "we" don't actually know what these images "mean," that to begin to apprehend their meaning "we" would actually have to talk to some of the spiritual people who show up from time to time (usually when "we" are not there) and place "ourselves" in the position of students. To avoid this troubling reversal of the normal political/knowledge hierarchy, science has created a set of explanatory devices that will give "us" every appearance of learned knowledge: categorization and counting.

There are many kinds of sites that have a sacred value to Begade Shutagot'ine. These include—if not most importantly, certainly most famously—the story-layered landscapes that echo a time when the world was new. They include the historical traces of the political struggles of Begade Shutagot'ine from times past, such as the posts put up around the Begade, around Caribou Flats by Chief Albert Wright. They include the graves of grandmothers and grandfathers, the places where the remains of those who came before can still be found. Is the place where the bear gets its power a sacred site? Certainly to the bear. Are the places that have been camped at by Begade Shutagot'ine year in and year out sacred? These are everyday use sites, but repeated everyday use over many years itself confers a certain status on a site. Are the mountains, the rivers, the bush themselves sacred? I think so, and I think Gabe and Paul thought so. In a world where these kinds of places become increasingly rare, it is perhaps the case that they grow more sacred by the day.

Extinguishment Plus Exhaustion
Equals Certainty Plus Termination (e + e = c + t)

The work with Begade Shutagot'ine gave me an insight into the "certainty" policy of the federal government respecting modern treaties. Currently there are two approaches to achieving certainty. The older approach is to have an Indigenous people extinguish their Aboriginal title in exchange for other "defined" benefits. The most recent approach is not to use the words "cede," "release," "surrender," or "convey," but rather to take a more affirmative though also more totalizing approach: the treaty agreement will be seen to fully and comprehensively "exhaust" an Indigenous signatory's Aboriginal rights. Russell Diabo, a friend and brilliant Mohawk policy analyst, calls this whole spectrum of policies and processes the "termination" agenda.

This may be seen as a recent version of what Marx (1977) called "primitive accumulation." By primitive accumulation, Marx described an historic process that led to the development of the initial forms of capital as abstract wealth. Primitive accumulation involved the use of force, state intervention, in ensuring that massive wealth surpluses could accumulate and provide the necessary investment sums to cover the start-up costs of capitalism. But the most basic, and for Marx the most important, element of primitive accumulation was separating the people from their access to the means of subsistence, thereby creating what Marx called "free, rightless" workers by ensuring that those workers could not provide for themselves. Dependence and reliance on others is a founding tenet of capitalist social relations. David Harvey (2003) has noted that primitive accumulation is not a stage of capitalism that belongs to the past; rather, it is a process and set of tools that capitalism continues to deploy: accumulation by dispossession. His analysis looks at the second Iraq war through this lens. Those Indigenous peoples around the world who confront global capital also face the logic of primitive accumulation.

Paradoxically, it is perhaps better to describe the Canadian state as primitive in its relations with Begade Shutagot'ine than the Begade Shutagot'ine themselves. Certainty means establishing control over the land so that it is available for purposes of capital accumulation. A by-product of this is creating dependent peoples, proletarianization: turning once self-sufficient, independent, self-reliant peoples into dependent wage workers without any strong, materially grounded, distinct identity, so they will be willing to go wherever they are required by capital. This is called "freedom" by the intellectual servants of the establishment. Ties to the land are, in other words, very inconvenient to the new world order.

People have perhaps always struggled against having their ties to the land severed. The historian E.P. Thompson had a few things to say about that struggle in early modern England, for example. For the most part, with occasional exceptions that are usually temporary, people who fight for their land have almost always lost. To see such loss as inevitable is one of the tools of the cheerleaders of capitalism; it helps if one can demoralize the enemy. Any victories against dispossession have been temporary because of the fact that totalization is unrelenting; it is a structural feature of contemporary society and will not stop until it is forced to stop by a fundamental social transformation: a revolution in the manner in which property relations are organized, a revolution that takes the well-being and dignity of people as greater in importance than the well-being of capital, a revolution not premised on the brilliance of this or that leader but rather on the social genius of communities and of community itself, a revolution in the streets the households the dance clubs the galleries the bedrooms and the back roads, the mountains the thresholds the jails, a revolution in the solidity of personal identities, a revolution in the structure of language allowing for the speaking of impossible ideals, a revolution capable of qualitative ethical distinctions, a revolution that treats ecology as a part of the self, a revolution that recognizes the fact that important decisions about the environment about people will take a long time and much discussion, a revolution that will allow distinctiveness and be decentred and unhomogenizing in its orientation, a revolution that knows itself knows what it is. Such an event will look to hunting peoples in the world as one source of inspiration.

The bush elders of northern Canada such as Paul Wright or Gabe Etchinelle did not demand a revolution. They simply wanted to prevent their lands from being taken away from them so that their grandchildren could in some manner live in a way that their grandparents had lived. But their complexly simple desire, and the values that their desire was based on, were in my view revolutionary in scope. The notion of property that Gabe and Paul circulated was not "we own it and we're not giving it up," but rather "we're willing to share it if we are respected." The premise of their view threatened the foundational logic of the established order. They knew when they weren't being respected. They were willing to stand up against those who treated them without respect. They gave the last years of their lives doing so.

The Grandparents

One time, in a living room in Tulita with me and Julia Harrison and Kimberly Harkness, a tape recorder running, Paul Wright said, "We practise our tradition because it is like saying thank you to our grandparents." "Saying thank you to our grandparents" runs directly against the grain of enlightenment notions of progress, where the grandparents and any other representatives of "tradition" are what is in the way, reminders of outdated, stale, old-fashioned ways of doing things. Freedom means freedom from the fetters of tradition. Progress means change that inexorably casts away those fetters. This is one of the defining facts of modernism.

Where once tradition had an ironclad hold over people, now it is on the wane, clearly past being on the defensive and actually almost entirely off the map when it comes to reasoned debate. Reasoned debate, though, rarely if ever stops to sort out differences among different kinds of traditions. That some peoples had egalitarian traditions while others had patriarchal or other kinds of social hierarchical traditions is too complex a thought, implies too complex an ethics and politics to bother with. With the pendulum of history now swung so far in favour of enlightenment progress, perhaps it is time to suggest that there may be some elements of tradition worthy of consideration. The idea that different traditions may suggest different values, that examination of the substantive practices embodied by different traditions may provide important social dividends may be due its brief day in the light of reason.

Progress comes with heralds pronouncing the benefits of the newness of the new. This, closely allied with fashion as it is, is a structural feature of the dominant culture. Each new commodity developed has its own advertising campaign, its own cheerleaders, its own trumpeters. The commodity system relies heavily on the newness of the new, otherwise it would be entirely possible that people would become unduly attached to the old, and this would pose a crisis for capital accumulation. Every soft drink must be new. Every model car must represent a radical break with the past. Soon we will have to suffer with six rotating blades on our disposable safety razors: imagine the advertisements for that! Historical materialists do well to stake a careful distance from the newness of the new. Walter Benjamin knew enough to expend enormous energy carefully examining the recently old for all that it said about capitalist culture. The newness of the new, though, has seeped even into the production of critical social theory: what will this year bring from the spring fashion catalogue of cultural criticism?

Paul Wright, a grandparent himself, thanked his grandparents by doing things, as much as possible, the way they did things, the way they taught him to do things. Practising his tradition, still a matter of choice for him, was a way of walking in his grandparents' shoes, repeating their motions, thanking them for the life they laboured to give him, embodying their teachings and their values. Repetition is an epistemological key to traditional cultures and marks a vast distance from the progress-accumulation narrative that underpins contemporary social forms in dominant cultures. Perhaps Paul thanked his grandparents because they gave him life, perhaps because they embedded a set of values in his marrow, perhaps because, among the relations that came with him and that would come after him, the ones who came before make a call that has a certain priority within Begade Shutagot'ine culture. There are those who barely begrudge their grandparents the social security that might allow them to live out their last days with a minimum measure of material well-being, of dignity. These are not Begade Shutagot'ine. Begade Shutagot'ine, as with many other gathering, fishing and hunting peoples and bush peoples, as befits the repetition logic that underpins "tradition," exhibit great respect for their elders—old-fashioned and outdated as they may be. "In" fashion, riding the crest that carries the newest of the new: here is something that deserves our suspicion, whether in clothing, biotechnology, or even social theory. "We practise our tradition because it is like saying thank you to our grandparents."

Gabe's Handshake

In 1998 I received word that Gabe Etchinelle was on his deathbed. He had been brought back to Tulita from southern hospitals to die. I travelled up to see him one last time, one of many many people who did so. I stayed with the Etchinelle family; Theresa and David were shaken during those days, about to face something almost inconceivable, life without "Granpa Gabe." Gabe was put up in a small house near the main road along the river. Outside the house a steady crowd of visitors shifted positions; food was constantly being brought, cooked, served. Large urns of tea and coffee were always ready. The community itself was holding watch. At some point, the day after my arrival, I was taken for a visit.

Much of the time, I was told, Gabe was asleep, marshalling his energies for the last minutes or perhaps for the journey to come. When I went in he was lying flat on the bed, face up, so emaciated-thin. But he was awake. There was a glint of recognition in his eye when he saw me, a hint of a smile. There was nothing for either of us to say. I sat quietly beside him with a few others. The room was thick with the smell of sickness, the staleness of near death. There was weeping and hushed tones. The light was dim, a blanket covered the window. People came and went. Some prayed in Christian manner. At some point Gabe asked for, I think, and got some drumming. Paul mostly sat quietly at Gabe's side, sometimes coming outside for a breath of air, to chat, to eat: sadness doubly etched on every line in his face. Gabe's words were low, someone would bend an ear closely to his lips to catch the few he offered. His breath rasped, each one seemed to come from far away carrying a great burden.

Later that summer I would go with Paul to Drum Lake. He never said anything but you could tell that losing Gabe was too much for him: there was no one left to share old stories with, to fight the battles with. Without Gabe, life started to become unbearable, I think, for Paul.

On one of my visits over the next few days, Gabe reached over and took my hand. We shook. His grip was surprisingly firm: even in those final days hours minutes, some of the strength of years of life on the land stayed with him; he was tough to the end. Death had to fight for him. Then his time stopped.

He had been a hunter, a great hunter, who lived much of his life in the Mackenzie Mountains, looking after himself, his family, other people who needed him. He had been an uncle, a grandpa, a friend to many. He had piloted the last moose-skin boat built by his people.

He had so much bush knowledge that even at the end, young men watched him to learn. He read the land like I read books. He fought against injustice and wanted better things for his people. He thought one mountain was worth far more than $80 million. He looked down on no one. He was kind to many who probably didn't deserve his kindness. He lived and died like the mountain man he was.

Gabe Etchinelle was Begade Shutagot'ine.

Paul's Funeral

In the fall of 1999 I received word that Paul had taken a turn for the worse, that he had at most a week or two to live. Some part of me didn't want to believe it. I put off travelling to Tulita for a week. Then for two. I was in the midst of another of the endless battles I fought and lost at Trent University: I was resigning in protest as department head, giving speeches at city hall, attending packed evening meetings, negotiating on all sides, thinking of launching court challenges, tallying up friends and foes and foes who became friends and friends who became foes. Caught up in so many things that I lost sight of my priorities, of what really matters. Then it was three weeks. Then four. Then David called again to tell me that Paul was gone.

About a year and a half before then, I had lost my own father. I stood across from the bed and watched him die in my brother's arms. The problem for me with working with elders is that I relive the experience of losing my own parent. I become attached closely to the elders I respect; they become parent-like figures for me. Psychologically, this is called transference. It happens. Paul, in the too-short time that I had with him, had become like a father to me. But they are older people, and they too will likely die before me. And I will experience their death, and I will experience the loss of them, and through the tears of mourning that I cry into the dirt I throw on their graves I will wonder again whether it was worth it. Every elder I meet and work with means I have accepted the fact that I will have more work of mourning to do.

Unlike with my father, unlike with Rosie Okpik, with Pauloosie Angmarlik from Panniqtuuq, unlike with Gabe Etchinelle, I never was able to say goodbye to Paul while he still lived. We parted after the trip to Drum Lake with plans of seeing each other again the next year. There was no next year.

I flew up to Tulita when I got the second phone call. It was all I could do. There were so many people there. It was a Denendeh who's who: important politicians, elders from other communities, Dene cultural activists. Paul Andrew was there and read the eulogy. We looked at each other like men, as if we now had to really be men for the first time, holding back or not holding back the tears. We were not built to sustain this.

There was a feast. There were drums. A grave was dug into the frozen earth. The sky was crisp and blue but may as well have been black for all we noticed.

At the feast, amidst the people wandering around, the talk, the kids running until hushed to stillness for a few minutes before they started up again, George Blondin stood up. He said a few words. He was glad to see so many people. This was how it used to be in the old days. It was good people had properly gathered in this way. It was good so many had come. It was good.

Paul Wright. Nephew of a great Begade Shutagot'ine chief named Albert Wright. A chief himself. A hunter. A father and a grandfather. A gifted leader. A gifted speaker. A devoted husband. A kind man with a twinkle in his eye. A maker of videos. A storyteller. A deeply spiritual man. A fighter for justice. A man who did not believe that lines on a map solved anything. A lover of the land. A man who could not easily pass a hungry person on the street. A troubled honest compassionate wise man.

Paul Wright was Begade Shutagot'ine.

DEPOSITION FOUR
Stewart Lake

How to stop a story that is always being told? Or, how to change
a story that is always being told? The story that settler-colonial
nation-states tend to tell about themselves is that they are new; they
are beneficent; they have successfully "settled" all issues prior to
their beginning. If, in fact, they acknowledge having complicated
beginnings, forceful beginnings, what was there before that process
occupies a shadowy space of reflection; it is allowed a blue future
life in cinematographic narratives such as *Avatar*; a ghostly prior
life in horror films, and a deeply regulated life in law and economic
distribution. Indians, or Native people, are not imagined to flourish,
let alone push or interrupt the stories that are being told.

—AUDRA SIMPSON

Aboriginal rights present the uncharted, the unknown,
and the unfamiliar to Canadian courts, politicians, political
thought, and Canadians. First Nations jurisprudences challenge the
self-congratulatory paradigm of Eurocentrism and
Eurocentric concepts of law with a distinct normative theory
previously extrinsic to or outside of Eurocentric law.

—JAMES YOUNGBLOOD HENDERSON

Hiatus

In the years after Paul Wright and Gabe Etchinelle passed away, the Sahtu Treaty was slowly implemented. Regional land use and water use and environmental boards were established in the Sahtu region. Nearby communities began to negotiate self-government agreements pursuant to the treaty. As the construction of the Mackenzie gas pipeline waxed and waned, there was a good deal of activity and some concern among Dene that the Sahtu Treaty was not as strong an instrument to protect their interests as they had hoped.

Among Begade Shutagot'ine, slowly a new generation moved into place as elders. David Etchinelle became recognized as chief of the Begade Shutagot'ine. After a pause of several years, I began travelling back to Tulita to read this text over to David and Theresa. With them I travelled to their home at Stewart Lake, and up the Redstone River to a sacred waterfall, and up the Begade to Sheep Mountain, seeing more and more of the land and hearing more and more of the stories. Although what I have written here is directed, however obliquely, at the project of reaffirming their land rights, my time with Begade Shutagot'ine has also helped me gain purchase or insight into broader issues around the nature and affirmation of Aboriginal rights. And perhaps in some small way, into the nature of the postmodern, dominant culture and society.

Slowly they draw me back into the struggle of Begade Shutagot'ine; they remind me what is at stake. I watch their courage as they refuse to sign on to the Sahtu Treaty, are denied benefits and potential jobs over a principle that may never be recognized, are treated in some ways as second-class citizens in their very small community of Tulita, yet remain proud to be carrying on the struggle of Paul and Gabe, of doing what their own elders advised them to do: standing up. In my newer set of travels I bring along research assistants—Agnes Pawlowska and Emily Grafton and Les Sabiston; friends and former students—Tee Lim, Peter Lichtenfels; and family members—my then partner Jaime Drew, my daughter Malay Pilz. I bring David and Theresa to the south, where we conduct formal interviews, and David travels with me to activist meetings of the Defenders of the Land activist network in Vancouver and near Halifax.

Instead of a footnote, an endnote, an epilogue, this new part of their struggle demands a new deposition, new stories, more reflection: it has become a part of the story of a people who tried to fight for their land, who are still fighting for their land.

Eagle Drops a Fish

Tulita is a long way away. In the midst of the hiatus, my base of operations changes from Trent University in Peterborough, Ontario, to the University of Manitoba in Winnipeg. This means that in three long days I can drive to Fort Simpson. That allows me to bring students and other witnesses while still marshalling my research funds to allow for bush travels. The drive takes us across the northern plains through Saskatoon to Edmonton, then up to either High Level or Fort Nelson, then to Fort Simpson and finally, the last few hours and last ferry to Pehdzi'ki (formerly Wrigley). From there David will meet us by boat and take us back downstream to Tulita.

One time we travel from Pehdzi'ki to Tulita through wind and rain, the boat hugging the shores of the Deh Cho to avoid the largest of the wind-whipped waves that could easily swamp us. It's slow going, fairly cold and very late, and dusk slowly sneaks the daylight away. There is a moment: our boat is travelling alongside an eagle that had seconds earlier snagged a fish from the river. The eagle is flying at nearly the same speed as the labouring boat, flying parallel and trying to gain height; but not fast enough, not high enough. The boat is too close for comfort. The eagle lets go of the heavy fish that is weighing it down and swoops away, upwards, behind the bank, out of sight, gone. Gone before any of us can pull out a camera. Gone before we have time to point it out to each other. A moment that charges the boredom of travel with an energy, a moment that disappears even more quickly than it arrives: perhaps this is what Walter Benjamin means by "now-time."

I've seen many many eagles. I have even seen an eagle swoop down to the Sahtu Deh (Bear River) and come up with a fish-feast writhing in its claws. But for some reason the eagle I remember most is that one, one of the closest I've ever been next to outside of a zoo: I remember because our boat, having to hug the shore, caused it to lose its feast, to lose however many hours and tries, however much patience and diligence it had spent catching its prey. I remember it not for the glory of seeing it but for the regret of having in a small way caused it harm. For to Begade Shutagot'ine we are all related: our ethic extends to land and waters, to animals, to birds, to fish. I owe an ethical debt to the eagle that dropped its fish, one I can never repay.

Outside the Governance Machine

In working with the Begade Shutagot'ine, from the time of Paul Wright's first invitation through my later work with Theresa and David Etchinelle, I was putting myself off to the side of the institutional systems of political engagement. This was not working with and for a band council or First Nations governance body in struggle; working with Begade Shutagot'ine involved being at least implicitly critical and sometimes in direct confrontation with various Sahtu-based authorities and governance mechanisms. To be fair, the local Tulita leadership never seemed to begrudge or question my presence; when Frank Andrew was chief he remained gregariously welcoming to me. There have been other communities and nations where that degree of tolerance for political dissent was not nearly so prevalent.

One of the changes in Denendeh over the past few decades has been the desire and ability of the range of Dene governance bodies to actually, actively, act as a political voice for bush families. The governance bodies themselves have come to require a degree of Western education that starts to mark a class of non-land-based leaders. The Sahtu Treaty created a leadership group dedicated to "economic development," invariably defined as "growing the capital pool," for whom bush families represent an obstacle.

In the heady days of the early 1970s, it was the chief and councils who fought for the land. Paul Wright's campaign toward the end of his life represented an attempt to maintain that land-based ethos in the face of a leadership group that had a different set of priorities. By the time I came to work with David and Theresa Etchinelle, the new institutional political structure had largely ossified: a professional leadership class of politicians who could speak in mainstream sound bites and technicians whose concern was for institutional credibility in modernist terms had come to dominate community life. The agency of the state as a distinct totalizing force casts its shadow in precisely this way: creating mini-states that can address it in the appropriate state-sanctioned forms, promoting social elites who become dependent on the institutional structure for their livelihood, and thereby recognizing forms it has always already known because they are nothing but its own forms. This is how a culture is eviscerated.

The Canadian state still cannot talk to or listen to bush people. Nor does it want to. It must exclude or contain them. Many years ago Gayatri Chakravorty Spivak wrote an essay noting that in the debate between national anti-colonialists (who may have relied in part on their distinct traditional cultures) and colonial capitalists (whose agenda flew under the flag of modernism), the voices of colonized women have been structurally excluded. Spivak herself drew inspiration from Karl Marx's discussion of the poor in his essay on Louis Bonaparte, in which he said of the very poor that "they cannot represent themselves, they must be represented" (1974). The institutional battles now taking place between the Canadian state and Indigenous authorities have also—not entirely but largely—come to a pass in which the voice of bush peoples is excluded or at most paid token attention, because in general it does not produce utterances that conform to the formal structures of speech that will underlie policy development. For these reasons, those Indigenous and non-Indigenous activists who work with bush people often find themselves working outside the Indigenous governance institutions.

Stewart Lake I: Getting There

Four days of travel gets us to Tulita, but Tulita has become a staging ground. We spend a few days there getting groceries and gas and bush gear ready, finalizing our plans based on money, weather, boats, planes. There is usually a drum dance or hand games to take part in. And I visit friends, most of whom have signed on to the Sahtu Treaty, so our conversations always have something of a mutually wary quality: everyone knows I'm working with and for David and Theresa. And David and Theresa are living, vocal reminders that the Sahtu Treaty is a land surrender. In this phase of my research the bush destination is almost always the Etchinelles' camp at Stewart Lake.

The first time we take a bush plane, landing on the lake but across from where the camp is; the lake is too shallow for the plane to reach the dock at the camp. So the plane gets unloaded and leaves, while we ferry in a motorboat back and forth to the camp. There is a cabin, some platforms for other cabins, a storage shed. There is a surprising range of supplies that have been hauled in by helicopter or in winter with snowmobiles: a small diesel generator probably shouldn't be a big surprise, but a working old-fashioned wringer washer seems improbable.

On other trips we get to Stewart Lake by jet boat, travelling upstream on the Deh Cho to the Begade, then up the Begade, past Red Dog Mountain, to the mouth of the creek that connects Stewart Lake to the Begade. From there we ride on all-terrain vehicles or on the trailers they pull, or we make the long walk, eventually reaching a cut line or trail that connects the creek to the camp site. David and Theresa and various children set up in the cabin, we set up in a storage shed or in a canvas-wall tent, with a little wood stove for warmth and spruce boughs on the ground.

Stewart Lake is less impressive than Drum Lake: it's smaller, shallower, and located at the foot of the mountains, not amidst them. It's not sheep country. From a winter hunting perspective, though, it's ideal: not too far from Tulita by snowmobile, a good way stop on the journey to Drum Lake or a good base camp. It has its own bush charm.

We arrive, drink some tea, secure our baggage, set up a place to stay, unpack, chop some wood, start a fire in our tent or shack. After four days of travel by car and boat to get to Tulita, after a couple of days of organizing people and boats and planes in town, after a day of travel on the river or by float plane, we arrive in Stewart Lake and settle in. We're ready.

Stewart Lake II: Being There

A small wooden dock. A clearing with a few plywood buildings scattered around, some tent frames and meat-drying racks, piles of firewood, a straight cut line or trail that connects to the creek, the hum of the diesel generator punctuating the caws or chirps of the birds. One morning a moose is spotted and hunted before I even wake up. Another day during a walk with Jaime along the trail, a black bear gets between us and the camp. One time there are porcupines nearby and all the dogs have to be kept tied up.

Husky Oil has been in the area, testing for oil or natural gas deposits. There's a grown-over landing strip—like the one at Caribou Flats but even less used—just behind the camp, though I never saw it used. Husky will sometimes help David and Theresa with their helicopters, hauling in supplies. Other times both parties keep a watchful distance. Stewart Lake is generally out of the way; there are never surprise visitors there the way there can sometimes be on the river.

In between hunting trips and stories there's the odd excursion: trying to catch fish in the deep water off the point (mostly we are there too early in August for the good fishing) or going swimming at the same spot, looking through deep bush for an old shelter David had built and stayed in on a hunting trip when he was younger, canoeing down the fast stream that feeds out of Stewart Lake and realizing that we'd have to return against the current, being shown the place where Wolverine first appears and that grand story cycle begins, slowly getting to know the contours of the northwest corner of the lake.

When the work of the day is done, I spend time in the cabin with a video camera on David; he tells the stories best in his own language and has lots of stories to tell. We talk about what is to be done to create a distinct Begade Shutagot'ine band. We talk about how the Sahtu Treaty is not working to protect the land and about the various meetings David has attended in the past year.

Sometimes in the afternoon David piles the kids onto a trailer and whips them around the camp in an all-terrain vehicle. Their laughter and chatter is one of the constants in camp. As is the repeated sound of methodical wood chopping, or the louder buzz of the power saw cutting up logs. It's cold enough at night that we keep the fire going, and warm enough in the day that hours can be spent in a T-shirt. There aren't many mosquitoes, but a lot of wild cranberries. On the creek we scare up ducklings. Tomorrow we'll go hunting.

In Praise of the All-Terrain Vehicle

Although once in a while a moose or caribou appears within sight of the Stewart Lake camp, at this time of year the caribou are mostly in the foothills, so we have to go to them. We go there by riding all-terrain vehicles (ATVs). The little four-wheelers are used all across the mid and far north. Normally they are used in towns by families that don't have a car or truck; in the Kivilliq communities in Nunavut there are ATV trails that lead to family cabins far off on the land. At Stewart Lake the bush is dense, so the ATVs follow trails cut wide enough for them in the bush. But mostly, the trails lead to creeks or streams or little rivers, which the ATVs make use of as highways.

To get from Begade to Stewart Lake, one rides up the creek on an ATV; to get from Stewart Lake into the foothills where the caribou are, one rides along the trail to the creek, then up and up and up the creek to its sources in the high hills. Often, the ATV will pull a trailer.

The creek is on a boulder, rock, sand, and gravel bed. Mostly rocks. It widens or narrows, with channels that split and combine. The creek marks a clearing in the bush, with spruce on both sides, though the creek bed is often quite wide (as much as 100 metres, as little as ten). The ATVs make their own path along this bumpy landscape. They cross and criss-cross the creek itself, the water sometimes coming far up the fat, thickly threaded tires, so that we riders lift our feet to keep them dry, hanging on tightly, wondering and worrying about tipping over and into the bitter cold water.

The first time I made this trip I thought it was madness: "These Dene are just crazy," I said to myself as we wound around another bend and splashed into another crossing, over another rock pile. David drove and I rode behind him. On other trips, and most of the time, I rode in the trailer being pulled behind. This was even more uncomfortable, as the trailer seemed determined to let me know the full extent of every single bump. The ride from the cabins to the hunting hills took longer than two hours: two hours of bumping, creek-crossing, grinding, smashing, bouncing, exhausting, exhilarating travel, two hours that carved themselves in pain into the fibre of my back.

Very few people in the south use ATVs in this way. They are usually recreational vehicles, occasionally assisting with work. Here at Stewart Lake, they are essential, and they are put through their paces. What would be a full day's walk becomes a few hours' ride. The ATVs allow hunters to carry heavy loads of meat back to camp. Begade Shutagot'ine hunters have found a friend in these noisy, rough little all-purpose machines.

A Caribou Hunt with Malay

One time my daughter Malay (then nine years old) and I made the trip from Stewart Lake to the foothills with three ATVs loaded with people and gear, pulling trailers. Far up the creek, it splits as each part reaches up to its headwaters in the foothills. There we had a fire and made tea and ate snacks, the journey ended, the hunting about to begin. David had gone further up the creek to the right; Malay and I stayed with James Etchinelle and his family to explore the rising hills that fed the creek to the left. Malay and I decided to start walking, getting a head start on the steep climb as James finished his tea and cigarettes.

As we walked I noticed fresh caribou tracks in the soft mud beside the creek. That made me more alert than I otherwise might have been. As we walked over the crest of a first ridge we saw caribou across a gully, on the next ridge. Slowly, making no sudden motions, we walked backwards out of sight. We tried waving to our friends far below us but they didn't appear to notice. So I sent my little girl—with far more energy than me!—to run back and let everyone know the caribou were close. As she got about two-thirds of the way back to our picnic spot, James started the ATV, put his youngest son

Pierre in the front with him, and starting driving up, Malay having turned around and with a couple of the boys running behind him. Pierre and James passed me to my left, trying to get higher than the animals. Then he stopped the machine and walked over to where he could get a shot. Malay, breathless, came staggering back, having run most of the way down and then back up. We carefully worked our way back over the ridge to where we could get a view.

The pause: the half-breath moment of anticipation immediately before the rupture.

The crack of the shot, the many motions: caribou running, James repositioning himself, us standing and moving to get a better look, another shot, caribou disappearing back over the higher ridge. We run up to James, who asks us to look after little Pierre as he goes in chase, and we slowly work our way down and up to the crumpled caribou. We'll have fresh meat on this day.

Up the Redstone River

Stewart Lake was not the only place Theresa and David showed me, though it became the headquarters for this second phase of my research. One summer some hunters had come back from a trip up the Redstone River asking questions about a strange waterfall they had seen far upriver. After some discussion, Begade Shutagot'ine elders from Tulita remembered this as a special place, a spiritual place. There was a woman spirit in these falls. Theresa decided she wanted to see it for herself, to gather some healing water from this source. So with James and Theresa's brother Michael Widow, Jaime and I set out by jet boat up the Deh Cho, past the Begade to another winding mountain river, the Redstone.

It took a long, full day, going against the current of the Deh Cho and against the faster current of the Redstone, stopping for tea, constantly keeping an eye out for moose, before we closed in on our destination. As the boat twisted deeper into the mountains we suddenly found ourselves in a canyon, sheer black cliffs on each side of us: the landscape alive with a new energy, a new beauty.

The canyon was a kind of gateway, and within half an hour of passing through it we were setting up our tents a short way across and downstream from our destination.

Sacred Sites III

The next morning after breakfast we made the short boat ride and the longer, forty-minute hike up to the falls. The waterfall itself was no more than four or five metres high, spilling white watery threads over a golden limestone base to the first of three large, terraced pools, almost like giant steps up to the falls. In and beside the splashing waters of the falls is the outline of an elderly face. Perhaps. From the vantage of the falls we had a clear view of the whole valley we were in, past the canyon.

We drank and gently washed in the water. We left bullets and coins and matches and tobacco in gratitude. We sat alone with our thoughts in quiet contemplation. We took some water in our water tins or glass jars. We took the perennial pictures. Somehow being at that place lent our every gesture a graceful quality. Time had slipped from its serial logic, had fallen from the timepieces, and we were left in an extended meditative moment accompanied by the lively sound of the little falls.

The grand, sweeping view of the valley. The extraordinary "presentation" of the glowing, golden, step-like terraces that pool below the falls. The touch of the spray, the coldness of the water. All this seemed to mute our conversation, turn us inward, and, perhaps, leave us feeling renewed, better in some strange incalculable way. One could only leave that time and place regretfully, tearing oneself away but still carrying a quality of contentment.

In Practice

The notion or concept of practice has been revived in recent times, in part because of Diana Taylor's influential definition of performance as "embodied practice." In an older tradition of thought, practice, productive activity, and praxis were all key terms in a dialectical understanding of the world that owed something to Marx's "Theses on Feuerbach." In Canada, when the Supreme Court finally came to the point of having to define Aboriginal rights, it said that Aboriginal rights are "customs, practices or traditions integral to the distinctive cultures of the people claiming the right." Practice now has a legal as well as conceptual status in Canada.

Much of what is described in this text can be understood as a reflection on the contemporary practices of Begade Shutagot'ine: hunting, fishing, storytelling, travelling, camping, butchering, feasting, hiking, searching, reconnecting. These practices, which draw on ancient practices, are now engaged in using newer forms of technology on a distinct, clearly defined territory. Some of the practices engage and articulate values: respecting, sharing, community building, struggling, resisting, reviving. A web of connections embedded in these practices ties Begade Shutagot'ine to their land and to each other. A machinery of coercive and consensual forces works insidiously and brutally to sever these connections and end these practices.

Taylor's work calls attention to the body as a fulcrum of practice, its site and destination, its animator. Totalization is a process of disembodiment and abstraction, relentlessly determining that decisions will be made based on quantitative factors with little or no relationship to the actual ground under our feet, or the unceded ground under the feet of Begade Shutagot'ine. It is impossible to deeply understand Aboriginal rights unless one's body encounters and embraces, for some brief period of time, the embodied practices upon which those rights are grounded.

History Repeats Itself. Again / Signing the Begade

In this phase of research, David and Theresa also really showed me the Begade. We used it often to go to or return from Stewart Lake. We made trips to Sheep Mountain and I got to know the first stretch of the river quite well. Red Dog Mountain became a friend, and I heard the story of how the river long ago was squeezed through a small hole in the mountain, which had to be walked over until someone rode through and changed the course of the river to its present place along the foot of the mountain. From Sheep Mountain we hunted and travelled further upriver, to the Steamboat (an incongruously beautiful small rock and tree island in the middle of the river near Norman Simmons's cabin); eventually even to where the Natla silts up the Begade, where the Begade makes a sharp bend up toward Caribou Flats (the elbow). The further up the river one travels, the more the mountains close in, the more spectacular the views. And the better the hunting. Eventually, after a long river apprenticeship, I even returned to Caribou Flats.

One time, under David's instruction, we had signs made asserting the territorial ownership of the Begade Shutagot'ine. James and David and I, with two friends, Peter Lichtenfels and Tee Lim, travelled fast and far up the river, putting a sign near the mouth (at the first major camping spot upriver), putting a sign near Red Dog Mountain, putting another at Sheep Mountain, putting one on the Steamboat, and a last one near the Natla. The wording on the sign had been established by David and Theresa.

Unlike on other trips, we got a moose, as evening was settling on our second day and we were just south of Sheep Mountain. As we hurtled upriver in the jet boat, James and David saw a motion near a creek and shot the moose from the boat. We made camp there. We had already put up the first two signs. After butchering the moose and hanging the meat, we knew we'd have only a couple more days on the river: the meat would have to be taken back to town before it would spoil. There was no Theresa to make dry-meat on this trip. So the next day we left the meat hanging and in less than an hour were at the camping spot at Sheep Mountain, where we put up a sign and hunted two caribou (a mother and older calf) that crossed the river not far upstream.

That day we travelled further upriver, putting a sign up and going past the Steamboat, camping and now ignoring the occasional caribou herd we saw as we pressed onward the next day. And finally we made it to the elbow, a gateway guarding the last stretch to Caribou Flats, taking a brief pause before we spun the jet boat around and went back, landing across from the silty Natla and putting up a last sign. There, surrounded by stark rugged mountains, I remembered the work of Albert Wright. Would these signs matter to anyone? Would they make a difference? Would they cause outrage? Would they stand silently watching for more generations of Begade hunters, or would they be quickly bulldozed by a rise in the price of oil and natural gas? In that moment of not knowing it still felt as if we had helped do something Paul and Gabe would have approved of: a simple on-the-ground gesture that echoed clearly and plainly: a writing on the land, of the land.

The Trickster and His Loads

One day as we were camped out along the Begade, in the spot where we had hunted the moose, four of us trying to perch on the stumps and a camp chair by the fire, David casually mentioned to Peter and me that there weren't enough seats; maybe we should move that big rock, a boulder really, just below us down the bank up to our campsite. It would make a lovely seat. By that time, how could I have not known better? We dutifully went down and tried to shift the rock, just testing it to see how hard this task would be. It wasn't going to be easy. But we were up for it, two white guys eager to show they weren't afraid of contributing to the work of camp life. And then we saw David's broad smile and knew how absurd this whole idea was. Perhaps these tricks that add to our load remind us that we do have room to carry more, that our burdens do not exhaust us, that we have more effort inside us. Perhaps they just make us sheepish at our obvious stupidity, shaking our heads and wondering how far astray we can actually be led.

Ever Further

One time I was able to return to Caribou Flats. It was late summer, 2016, and on this trip David, James, David Jr., Lyle, and my friend and videographer Janet Sarson piled with me into the jet boat. In one very long day we made the trip from Tulita to Caribou Flats. We hunted caribou, including in the same spot where we found so many in 1997. We eventually saw sheep on the mountain behind our camp and went up to get them, one group of hunters only. They spotted us and ran away.

Some things had changed. Now we could manage to use satellite radio phones more effectively and were able to call back to town each day. Some things remained the same. The valley was as beautiful as it had always been: mountains flecked with the shadows of moving clouds. The hunters allowed the youngest team member, Lyle, to shoot all the caribou we got on that trip. One time David managed to fill my pack with the butchered meat of a caribou about a kilometre behind our camp, in the bush. When I lifted it I knew I was getting the heavy load. David Jr., who is strong and can carry huge loads, almost laughed when he saw how light his would be. I followed him back to camp, not stopping for a break, in my head cursing at David and very glad to get the pack off my back. The next day, in the same clearing, Lyle got another caribou. This time David Jr. took a heavy load and I got something more appropriate for my size. But for a moment, when they gestured to me to take up David Jr.'s pack, I thought "Oh no!" They were watching for my expression and all laughed heartily.

We set up more signs, going up as far as the Tuutsi River: further than I had ever been on the Begade. But looking at the clear water as the river split, trying to see as far upriver as my eyes would take me, I dreamed of going ever further, to the place where the giant beavers and giant panthers still roamed, to some other glorious configuration of mountain and river and valley, to another time and another way of being the laughter the dream the light the delirium and the persistent but fragile precarious and finite community of humans.

Time to Leave

The time comes when we must say goodbye to the Begade, the Deh Cho, Drum Lake, Stewart Lake, Tulita, Caribou Flats, raven and caribou and bear and sheep and porcupine, cranberries and blueberries, mushrooms and medicines, we say goodbye to the smell of spruce and the sound of the river. As we get on the float plane, the gravel strip plane, the jetliner, the boat, the four-wheel-drive SUV, we say goodbye to the stories and the drum songs, we say goodbye to feeding the river, feeding the land, feeding the fire, we say goodbye to the children and the elders to the youth to the women to the men, we say goodbye to a sun that circles the sky and to the sacred places it greets, we say goodbye to our own vital years of conversation and hope and love and mourning and laughter and shame and struggle, we say goodbye to the canvas-wall tents the unrelenting rains the steep climbs and crossing the creeks in ATVs—until finally we say goodbye to even the last lingering moment of a farewell that knows no end.

CLOSING BRIEF

Love Letter to Section 25 of the Canadian Constitution

We were pulling back into camp after six long hours of boating along the Begade, stopping here and there at islands to scour them for moose, climbing ridges to peer out into the back country, making a small fire for tea by the river. We had gone north and west, against the current, further and further and further. No moose. We passed places I hadn't seen in years, Simmons's cabin, the Steamboat. The twisted rust-red layers of sedimentary rocks that ran at crazy angles in cliffs beside the river, the mountains in the distance gave us plenty to picture. Finally we turned back, still hoping for a moose, somewhere, making the return trip to our camp at Sheep Mountain in about two hours. There were two jet boats with four or five people in each, all Dene except me and my two students, Les and Agnes. This took place in the later phase of this project, at the time when I renewed the work with David and Theresa. We returned to our camp empty-handed, exhausted but also delighted by what we had seen, having travelled up from Sheep Mountain to a place past Simmons's camp and the Steamboat. As we tied the boat the kids on the shore could hardly contain themselves. "Sheep!" they were yelling, "There's sheep across"; they had spotted mountain sheep, Dall sheep, on the mountain across from our camp. Off the beach and landing area, in the trees, were the tents and cooking fire. There were a few blackened wieners on the grill; I grabbed one and wrapped a slice of bread around it and shoved it into my mouth: it was gone in two sloppy bites. I was back at the boat within a couple of minutes. Les and Agnes, weary and having let themselves give in to tiredness, stayed back, not quite realizing that our hunting day was actually now beginning, not ending.

Five of us in one boat as we head almost straight across the river. Four hunters and me. We walk carefully along the shore on the other side, scanning for sheep, reaching a spot where we can see into the ravine to where the sheep had last been seen. High up on a ledge on a cliff, we make out a white spot. It's an awkward space to get at. James, the lead hunter, surveys the situation and makes a quick decision. The other three hunters will stay at the bottom, perhaps manoeuvre a bit up a slope to get the best shot they can, in case the sheep start to move. James will go up the avalanche slope in the next ravine and see if he can hike to where he's above the sheep, in which case our chances of getting them improve enormously. Almost casually, I ask James if I can follow him. "Sure," he says. So I start to climb over the tumbled stones and rocks into the ravine.

--·--·--·--·--·--·--·--

We walk up the rough jumble of rocks, climbing and climbing. My heart starts to pound and I remember that it's already been a long day in the boat, without too much food. I start to wonder whether it was wise of me to make this hike. But it's too late, I'm in it. And the excitement of possibly getting a sheep helps. In some places the terrain is so steep that I find myself crawling rather than walking. I'm glad for my new hiking boots. James stays about twenty feet ahead of me, rifle strapped to his back. My breathing gets a bit laboured, my heart pounding and pounding like a Dene drum. After a time—twenty minutes, thirty?—we hear shots, three shots, from below. The sheep must have started moving. We wait for a signal shot to call us down (me quietly hoping the hunters below were successful so I can just turn and head back—ahhhh). Nothing. We start moving up again. James sees something, swings the rifle around, tries to take aim, but he's unsteady on his feet. Rocks, mostly little stones but some a bit larger, jarred loose by the running sheep, are flying all around me and I'm batting them away. James can't shoot, loses sight of the sheep. I look up and on the ridge to my right get a brief glimpse of the head of a sheep, moving downwards and more to my right. I make it close to James and tell him what I saw. We decide to keep going up.

Ahead, also to our right, is a packed mud landslide slope; steeper, but it looks like we can hike it. As we get there we realize the mud is too densely packed. We have to climb up the rocky sides of the mud patch. James is ahead again, on the right side. In order to avoid the stones he jars loose, I start to climb up the left. Here and there I reach a ledge, test it with my weight, and end up pulling out a huge rock and letting it tumble below me. But my side has better handholds than James's, and I don't have a rifle, so I catch up to him. By now we are free climbing, straight up. We look across at each other, no words, but our eyes say, "This is crazy. We're such fools." Twice as we keep going up, closer to the top, we exchange these intense, wordless, "we must be crazy" glances. I've barely looked around, but can sense we're well up the mountain. By now I'm feeling some kind of adrenaline rush. My heart still pounds, I'm breathing heavy, but in spite of the long day I want to keep going, I want to get that damn sheep! We're stupid fools! Idiots! Ridiculous clowns! But we keep climbing, painstaking hand- and foothold after painstaking hand- and foothold.

—·—·—·—·—·—·—·—

I found working with David and Theresa a useful foil that allowed me to see the grand policies, court cases, constitutional documents, and agreements that I read as a matter of course in a more grounded way. One of the things I've learned, in part through my work with Begade Shutagot'ine, is that the Canadian Constitution

(1982), including both the Charter of Rights and Freedoms and section 35 on Aboriginal and treaty rights, actually represents a stronger philosophical position than the newly canonized 2007 United Nations Declaration on the Rights of Indigenous Peoples (UNDRIP). The UNDRIP basically is a document that enshrines the human rights of Indigenous peoples. Although some sections deal with Aboriginal rights, the declaration is not really a strong legal instrument for the protection of Aboriginal rights. It is not that UNDRIP is a step backwards; it is clearly the result of a long struggle by a generation of inspired Indigenous leaders. Or that Canada is so wonderful to its Indigenous people, as anyone paying attention to the story of the Begade Shutagot'ine—and so many others—can attest. And UNDRIP does contain very detailed and useful language that will contribute to global Indigenous struggles for land and dignity and justice. But Aboriginal rights are not human rights. They are the special rights that Indigenous peoples have by virtue of being the earliest occupants of a territory and practitioners of a distinct culture. They therefore have land and cultural rights, in Canada and elsewhere, that show an appreciation for their status. Canada has, in fact, been a world leader in articulating a doctrine of Aboriginal rights; though not in actually implementing that doctrine. And its status in law is protected by the famous section 35 of our Constitution, which "recognizes and affirms existing aboriginal and treaty rights." But it is section 25, often overlooked, that makes our Constitution a structural improvement over the United Nations Declaration on the Rights of Indigenous Peoples.

This structure needs to be in place because Indigenous peoples in Canada have a status over and above their status as equal citizens. Even official multiculturalism cannot properly accommodate such a status. For First Peoples, like Begade Shutagot'ine, there is no other homeland: no other place where their language dialect will be spoken, their stories told, their songs sung to the glorious rhythm of their drums; no other place where the caribou will be butchered in quite that way, where the fresh sheep ribs will have that explosive flavour, and where their ways of hunting or camping or feeling the passing of ephemeral moments in play, or strict discipline for children, or exhaustion after a day's travels or work or talk exist. My culture and languages, Polish and Ukrainian, thrive in other lands even if forgotten in my own body. So too do the cultures and languages of newcoming people from around the world who have made a home in Canada. But there is no other home for Begade Shutagot'ine or for any of the other Indigenous peoples of Canada. Equality rights cannot recognize this fact. Nor can an undifferentiated multiculturalism. Only Indigenous rights can provide a legal structure that grasps this material and cultural fact. And if Indigenous rights are housed under the umbrella of human rights, the grasp loosens. They become second-place rights, rights to uphold only when it is convenient.

Section 25 of the Canadian Constitution says that the Charter of Rights and Freedoms, the most powerful expression of human rights in Canada, will not be interpreted in a way that diminishes Aboriginal and treaty rights. It therefore puts both different forms of rights on something of an equal footing. It ensures that just because my Dene friends can hunt a duck in the springtime, as they have done since ancient times, I will not use equality provisions of the Constitution to engage in the same practice. Or, more likely, I will not say that all duck-hunting restrictions should be applied equally in accordance with the principle of the human right to equal treatment under law.

—·—·—·—·—·—·—·—

Climbing. Now it is a matter of a little movement upwards at a time. Resting. Searching out handholds or footholds. Climbing. Resting. I've gotten ahead of James. I'm close to the top. I can't go further on my side. James suggests that I cross the packed mud, which has narrowed to a metre-wide gap, to his side and see if there's a way up, over the top. He warns me that if I start to slide, bend one leg to try and control and slow myself. I kick out a smudge in the mud, reach over to find a grip, and swing myself over. From here I can see over the ridge. No sheep below us, where I had hoped to see them. There are no more handholds to help me up further. I now realize we are very high: I can see the river valley stretched out below us and the almost sheer drop we have climbed. Above me are a few dead branches. I can't grab them because they might come loose. The one live branch I can reach, barely, would swing me around, if it held, over the packed mud: no good. I look back down at James, who has crossed to "my" former side of the sheer cliff. "Nothing," I say, "nothing to grab on to." I can't go any further. Finally and regretfully he says, "We should go back down." If he had been on his own, no doubt he would have grabbed onto some branches and pulled himself up, but he won't take such a risk with me.

I'm relieved. I didn't want to risk making a mistake. So close and yet so far from the top, with no sheep in sight; it was time to turn back. Now I had my back to the mountain. I needed to make the step back across the mud slope, to "my" side, where James was, where I knew there were hand- and footholds and a treacherous but viable path to safety below. It wasn't going to be easy to make the crossing back, because now I was faced away from the mountain. I gulped, and tried to take the step in a smooth single motion that would have me across in no time. As I put my weight on my right leg I just felt things let go and started to skid, straight down, with stones and rocks and mud crashing around me, sliding, sliding . . .

— ᐧ — ᐧ — ᐧ — ᐧ — ᐧ —

Aboriginal peoples like my Dene friends enjoy human rights inasmuch as they are, after all, also human. In theory there is no need for an "extension" of human rights to them, since they have them already. Aboriginal rights, however, are another cup of tea altogether.

They are rights only enjoyed by Indigenous peoples, prior occupants of a land. In Canada, that means Ininew, Ojibway, Nisga'a, Inuit, Metis, and Dene, among many other First Peoples. But human rights can sometimes be used to destroy Aboriginal rights; the two do not live in benign cohabitation. In Canada in 1969 the federal government had tried to force "equality" on First Nations through the now infamous White Paper. A human right was used to try to curtail Aboriginal and treaty rights. After the White Paper was defeated the historical experience was burned into the consciousness of a generation of Canadian Indigenous leaders.

That's why, in the early 1980s when the Constitution was negotiated, along with a section that recognized Aboriginal rights, another section was written, this one a part of our Charter of Rights and Freedoms that is embedded within the Constitution. Section 25 said that none of the human rights and freedoms of the Charter would be interpreted in a manner that diminished Aboriginal rights. It was a brilliant solution to the problem and ensured that in Canadian law, Aboriginal rights would have equal status with human rights, or actually override human rights where they conflicted with Aboriginal rights. While we are still in the process of "defining and identifying" Aboriginal and treaty rights, as a nation we have a strong structure or foundation to work from. As I noted above in the brief section on practice, Aboriginal rights have come to be seen by Canadian courts as "practices, customs or traditions that are integral to the distinctive culture" of the people in question. An example of such a practice might be the sheep hunting of Begade Shutagot'ine at Sheep Mountain.

---·---·---·---·---·---·---

I've got one leg stuck out straight, another bent slightly under me, somehow managing to follow James's advice, so I'm partly controlling my slide. James had turned away and as he looks back I've dropped past him, sliding straight down. Rocks and gravel and dirt are sliding with me. A rock the size of a baseball hits the back of my head, but it must have just been dislodged (and I no doubt have a fairly thick skull); it had no momentum and doesn't hurt. Much.

Whenever the worst happens I grow very calm inside. In the moment when the bear pops up next to me or the dogs charge or the pepper spray spreads or the loving arms of the police wrap around me, I have no fear. Very soon after I may shake uncontrollably, but in the moment of action I am often calm. I'm trying to control my slide and thinking, "If those rocks below move when I hit them, this could be it." "It." The sheer slope is shaped in a way like a children's slide. It tails off. I think the whole slide was about twenty metres and only lasted a half minute or so. I hit the rocks and skid onto them. They stay firm. I turn around and start batting away the larger rocks and stones that have come down with me, until the last one bounces by.

James calls out. "I'm fine!" I yell out in reply, surprised that I'm not even shaky. I move gingerly over to the far side of this rock slope so that the stones James dislodges as he works his own way down won't whack me. He starts to pick his way down and I survey the damage. A bit of blood. Some scratches on my arm and hand. One of my knuckles is throbbing. Probably what will be a big bruise on my leg. Bits of stone everywhere in my jacket—some I will find months later when reaching a hand into the pocket of the same jacket while in London, England. It takes James almost twenty minutes to climb down that twenty-metre stretch, and he has to make a small jump at the end, perhaps a metre, but he lands solidly and safely, rifle intact. We bounce the rest of the way down the hill, from one rock to the next. I'm still tired and damn hungry, but somehow, feeling that if I can have this kind of adventure as a fifty-something professor, life, whose boundaries I had just poked, couldn't all be bad.

.—.—.—.—.—.—.—.

The next day we get a sheep, near the same spot. A few days after that Ethel Blondin-Andrew—former Liberal MP for the NWT—and her husband Leon show up at our camp. Ethel brings some dried meat and a lot of good cheer. We trade stories and catch up, sitting around the fire. David and Theresa are thinking about putting up some markers on various strategic bits of land along the Begade, asserting their continued stewardship, something we do a few years later (that trip is discussed in Deposition Four). For all of my disgust at the way the Begade Shutagot'ine are being treated, I've come to a strong sense that at least we in Canada have devised a constitutional structure that gives them hope. Certainly the Supreme Court of Canada has understood this issue and clearly stated that Aboriginal rights are, in our country, not to be diminished by universalist doctrines of human rights. What seals the deal is the often overlooked section 25, which sits there in the midst of the Constitution, kind of like the Steamboat, a beautiful river marker that reminds us of how powerful the river itself can be.

---·—·—·—·—·—·—·—·—·—·—·—·—

I would like to tell the story of a people who tried to fight for their land. It is the story of a chief, Albert Wright, who may or may not have signed a treaty but put up posts on his land to mark what belonged to his people. It is the story of two elders, Gabe Etchinelle and Paul Wright, who late in their lives tried to keep their people separate from a bureaucratic process that intended to sell their land. It is a story of a new generation of elders, David and Theresa Etchinelle, refusing to accept money and other benefits, standing up for strong principles they were handed by their own elders. It is a story that has taken place all across Canada, all across the Americas, each time with its own lineage its own permutation its own resolution. It is a story that continues to this day and that has no predetermined ending. These pages, these sentences, these words are now a small part of the story, one of its resting places or moments; it is a story I leave in your care.

ACKNOWLEDGEMENTS

Masi to many people who over many years helped with the research that led toward this book.

Masi cho to research assistants and former partners who travelled with me: Kim Harkness, Elizabeth Fajber, Jim Welch, Krista Pilz, Agnieszka Pawlowska-Mainville, Les Sabiston, Jaime Drew, Emily Grafton, Janet Sarson. I also thank Tee Lim and Peter Lichtenfels for joining me in 2014, and Jennifer Keith for other research support.

Masi cho to all my Dene hosts over many years: Paul Wright, Gabe Etchinelle, and Michael Widow, who are no longer with us, and Judith Wright, Fabien Bird, David Etchinelle, Theresa Etchinelle, James Etchinelle, Sean Etchinelle, Michael Etchinelle, David Etchinelle Jr., and everyone else from Tulita or elsewhere who joined us on our mad river and lake trips.

In the Inuit sky, *Akkutujuuk* are the two stars whose appearance signals the imminent return of the sun. My own little *Akkutujuuk* are named Malay Pilz and Josef Kulchyski-Drew, and my every breath is a *masi cho* to them. In the Winnipeg sky they have been joined by three other stars, Sarah Jacobson, Iris Jacobson, and thoughtful loveliness in human form, Jessica Jacobson-Konefall.

Masi cho also to the Social Sciences and Humanities Research Council, who sponsored this work over many years, first with a Standard Research Grant called "talking about the land: environmental and speech ethics among Begade Shutagot'ine," and most recently with an Insight Grant on "culture, law, politics, and history of Begade Shutagot'ine." The Manitoba Research Alliance has also supported this work with supplementary funds, and my work with them over many years has enriched and inspired me.

BIBLIOGRAPHY

Abel, Kerry. 1993. *Drum Songs: Glimpses of Dene History.* Montreal and Kingston: McGill-Queen's University Press.

Adorno, Theodor. 1991 [1951]. *Minima Moralia.* Translated by E.F.N. Jephcott. New York: Verso.

Agamben, Giorgio. 1998. *Homo Sacer.* Translated by Daniel Heller-Roazen. Stanford, CA: Stanford University Press.

———. 2013. *The Highest Poverty.* Translated by Adam Kotsko. Stanford, CA: Stanford University Press.

Alfred, Taiaiake (Gerald). 1995. *Heeding the Voices of Our Ancestors.* Don Mills, ON: Oxford University Press.

———. 2005. *Wasase.* Toronto: University of Toronto Press.

———. 2009. *Peace, Power, and Righteousness.* Don Mills, ON: Oxford University Press.

Arendt, Hannah. 1973. *The Origins of Totalitarianism.* New York: Harcourt, Brace, Jovanovich.

Asch, Michael. 1973. *Home and Native Land.* Toronto: Methuen.

———. 2014. *On Being Here to Stay.* Toronto: University of Toronto Press.

Asch, Michael, ed. 1997. *Aboriginal and Treaty Rights in Canada.* Vancouver: University of British Columbia Press.

Bagchi, Amiya. 2005. *Perilous Passage*. Toronto: Rowman and Littlefield.

Bannerji, Himani. 1995. *Thinking Through*. Toronto: Women's Press.

Barnaby, George. 1977. "The Political System and the Dene." In *Dene Nation: The Colony Within*, edited by Mel Watkins, 120–22. Toronto: University of Toronto Press.

Bell, Catherine, and Michael Asch. 1997. "Challenging Assumptions: The Impact of Precedent in Aboriginal Rights Litigation." In *Aboriginal and Treaty Rights in Canada*, edited by Michael Asch, 38–74. Vancouver: University of British Columbia Press.

Benjamin, Walter. 1978a. *Illuminations*. Translated by Harry Zohn. New York: Schocken Books.

———. "The Storyteller." 1978b. In *Illuminations*. Translated by Harry Zohn. New York: Schocken Books.

———. "Theses on the Philosophy of History." 1978c. In *Illuminations*. Translated by Harry Zohn. New York: Schocken Books.

Berger, Thomas. 1977. *Northern Frontier, Northern Homeland*, Vol. 1. Ottawa: Queen's Printer.

Berkes, Fikret. 2012. *Sacred Ecology*. New York: Routledge.

Blaser, Mario, Harvey Feit, and Glen McRea, eds. 2005. *In the Way of Development*. London: Zed Books.

Blondin, George. 1990. *When the World Was New: Stories of the Sahtu Dene*. Yellowknife: Outcrop.

———. 1997. *Yamoria the Lawmaker: Stories of the Dene*. Edmonton: NeWest Publishers.

Boldt, Menno. *Surviving as Indians*. 1993. Toronto: University of Toronto Press.

Boldt, Menno, and J. Anthony Long. 1985. "Tribal Traditions and European-Western Political Ideologies." In *The Quest for Justice*, edited by Menno Boldt and J. Anthony Long, 331–46. Toronto: University of Toronto Press.

Borrows, John. 2002. *Recovering Canada*. Toronto: University of Toronto Press.

Brody, Hugh. 1977. *The People's Land*. Harmondsworth, UK: Penguin Books.

———. 1983. *Maps and Dreams*. Harmondsworth, UK: Penguin Books.

———. 2000. *The Other Side of Eden*. Vancouver: Douglas and McIntyre.

Buck-Morss, Susan. 1989. *The Dialectics of Seeing*. Cambridge, MA: MIT Press.

Cairns, Alan C. 2000. *Citizens Plus: Aboriginal Peoples and the Canadian State*. Vancouver: University of British Columbia Press.

Canada, Government of. 1957. *Treaty No. 11*. Ottawa: Edmond Cloutier.

———. 1996. Report of the Royal Commission on Aboriginal Peoples, Vol. 2. *Restructuring the Relationship: Part One*. Ottawa: Minister of Supply and Services Canada.

———. 1996. Report of the Royal Commission on Aboriginal Peoples, Vol. 2. *Restructuring the Relationship: Part Two*. Ottawa: Minister of Supply and Services Canada.

———. 1996. Report of the Royal Commission on Aboriginal Peoples, Vol. 4. *Perspectives and Realities*. Ottawa: Minister of Supply and Services Canada.

———. 2003. *Resolving Aboriginal Claims: A Practical Guide to Canadian Experiences.* Ottawa: Minister of Indian Affairs and Northern Development.

Coates, Kenneth. 1985. *Canada's Colonies.* Toronto: James Lorimer.

Cole, Peter. 2006. *Coyote and Raven Go Canoeing.* Montreal: McGill-Queen's University Press.

Cornell, Drucilla. 1992. *The Philosophy of the Limit.* New York: Routledge.

Coulthard, Glen. 2014. *Red Skin, White Masks.* Minneapolis: University of Minnesota Press.

Cox, Bruce Alden, ed. 1988. *Native People, Native Lands.* Ottawa: Carleton University Press.

Cruikshank, Julie. 1990. *Life Lived Like a Story: Life Stories of Three Yukon Native Elders.* Vancouver: University of British Columbia Press.

———. 1994. "Claiming Legitimacy: Prophecy Narratives from Northern Aboriginal Women." *American Indian Quarterly* 18 (2): 147–67.

———. 2000. *The Social Life of Stories.* Vancouver: University of British Columbia Press.

Culhane, Dara. 1998. *The Pleasure of the Crown.* Burnaby, BC: Talon Books.

Cumming, Peter A., and Neil H. Mickenberg. 1971. *Native Rights in Canada.* Toronto: General Publishing.

Dacks, Gurston. 1981. *A Choice of Futures.* Toronto: Methuen.

Denendeh: A Dene Celebration. 1984. Yellowknife: The Dene Nation.

Derrida, Jacques. 1976. *Of Grammatology.* Translated by Gayatri Chakravorty Spivak. Baltimore: Johns Hopkins University Press.

————. 1992a. "Force of Law." In *Deconstruction and the Possibility of Justice*, edited by Drucilla Cornell, Michel Rosenfeld, David Gray Carlson, and translated by Mary Quaintance, 3–67. New York: Routledge.

————. 1992b. *Given Time: I. Counterfeit Money*. Translated by Peggy Kamuf. Chicago: University of Chicago Press.

————. *Specters of Marx*. 1994. Translated by Peggy Kamuf. New York: Routledge.

Diamond, Stanley. 1987. *In Search of the Primitive: A Critique of Civilization*. New Brunswick, NJ: Transaction.

Dickerson, Mark O. 1992. *Whose North?* Vancouver: University of British Columbia Press.

Fumoleau, René. 1973. *As Long as This Land Shall Last: A History of Treaty 8 and Treaty 11, 1870–1939*. Toronto: McClelland and Stewart.

Getty, Ian A.L., and Antoine S. Lussier, eds. 1983. *As Long as the Sun Shines and Water Flows*. Vancouver: University of British Columbia Press.

Green, Joyce, ed. 2007. *Making Space for Indigenous Feminism*. Winnipeg: Fernwood.

Habermas, Jürgen. 1979. *Communication and the Evolution of Society*. Translated by Thomas McCarthy. Boston: Beacon Press.

Haraway, Donna. 1991. *Simians, Cyborgs, and Women*. New York: Routledge.

Harvey, David. 1992. *The Condition of Postmodernity*. Cambridge, MA: Blackwell.

————. 2003. *The New Imperialism*. Toronto: Oxford University Press.

Heller, Henry. 2011. *The Birth of Capitalism*. Winnipeg: Fernwood.

Helm, June. 2002. *The People of Denendeh*. Montreal: McGill-Queen's University Press.

Henderson, James Youngblood. 2006. *First Nations Jurisprudence and Aboriginal Rights*. Saskatoon: University of Saskatchewan.

Horkheimer, Max, and Theodore Adorno. 1994 [1944]. *The Dialectic of Enlightenment*. Translated by John Cumming. London: Allen Lane.

Irlbacher-Fox, Stephanie. 2009. *Finding Dahshaa*. Vancouver: University of British Columbia Press.

Ivison, Duncan, Paul Patton, and Will Sanders, eds. 2000. *Political Theory and the Rights of Indigenous Peoples*. Cambridge: Cambridge University Press.

Jameson, Fredric. 1988. *The Political Unconscious*. Ithaca, NY: Cornell University Press.

———. 1991. *Postmodernism: Or, The Cultural Logic of Late Capitalism*. Durham, NC: Duke University Press.

Kulchyski, Peter. 1997. "From Appropriation to Subversion: Aboriginal Culture in the Age of Postmodernism." *American Indian Quarterly* 21 (4): 605–20.

———. 2005. *Like the Sound of a Drum*. Winnipeg: University of Manitoba Press.

———. 2007a. "hunting stories." In *The Culture of Hunting in Canada*, edited by Jean L. Manore and Dale G. Miner, 25–41. Vancouver: University of British Columbia Press.

———. 2007b. *The Red Indians*. Winnipeg: Arbeiter Ring Press.

———. 2012a. "bush/writing: embodied deconstruction, traces of community and writing against the state in indigenous acts of inscription." In *Shifting the Ground of Canadian Literary Studies*, edited by Smaro Kambuoreli and Robert Zacharias, 249–68. Waterloo, ON: Wilfrid Laurier University Press.

——. 2012b. "Echo of an Impossible Return: An Essay Concerning Fredric Jameson's Utopian Thought and Gathering and Hunting Social Relations." In *The Politics of the (Im)Possible*, edited by Barnita Bagchi, 47–61. London: Sage Publications.

——. 2013a. *Aboriginal Rights Are Not Human Rights*. Winnipeg: Arbeiter Ring Publishing.

——. 2013b. "'Speaking the Strong Words': Notes on Performing Indigenous Community Politics in Denendeh." In "Indigeneity and Performance: Interdisciplinary Perspectives," edited by Helen Gilbert. *Interventions: International Journal of Postcolonial Studies* 15 (2): 286–99.

——. 2015. "Trail to Tears: Concerning Modern Treaties in Northern Canada." *Canadian Journal of Native Studies* 31 (1): 69–81.

——. 2016a. "Bush Sites/Bush Stories: Politics of Place and Memory in Indigenous Northern Canada." *Profession* (online journal of the Modern Language Association), July. profession.mla.hcommons.org/2016/07/13/bush-sites-bush-stories-politics-of-place-and-memory-in-indigenous-northern-canada/.

——. 2016b. "Hunting Theories: Totalisation and Indigenous Resistances in Canada." *Historical Materialism* 24 (3): 30–44.

——. 2016c. "Rethinking Inequality in a Northern Indigenous Context: Affluence, Poverty, and the Racial Reconfiguration and Redistribution of Wealth." *Northern Review* 42: 97–108.

Kulchyski, Peter, and Warren Bernauer. 2014. "Modern Treaties, Extraction, and Imperialism in Canada's Indigenous North: Two Case Studies." *Studies in Political Economy* 93: 3–24.

Kulchyski, Peter, ed. 1994. *Unjust Relations: Aboriginal Rights in Canadian Courts*. Toronto: Oxford University Press.

Kuokkanen, Rauna. 2007. *Reshaping the University*. Vancouver: University of British Columbia Press.

LaCapra, Dominick. 1994. *Representing the Holocaust*. Ithaca, NY: Cornell University Press.

Larocque, Emma. 2010. *When the Other Is Me*. Winnipeg: University of Manitoba Press.

Leacock, Eleanor Burke. 1981. *Myths of Male Dominance*. New York: Monthly Review Press.

Leacock, Eleanor Burke, and Richard Lee, eds. 1982. *Politics and History in Band Societies*. Cambridge: Cambridge University Press.

Leopardi, Giacomo. 1984. *Pensieri*. New York: Oxford University Press.

Loxley, John. 2010. *Aboriginal, Northern, and Community Economic Development*. Winnipeg: Arbeiter Ring Publishing.

Lyotard, Jean-François. 1984. *The Postmodern Condition*. Translated by Geoff Bennington and Brian Massumi. Minneapolis: University of Minnesota Press.

Macklem, Patrick. 2001. *Indigenous Difference and the Constitution of Canada*. Toronto: University of Toronto Press.

Macpherson, C.B. 1965. *The Real World of Democracy*. Toronto: CBC Enterprises.

Manuel, Arthur, and Ronald Derrickson. 2015. *Unsettling Canada*. Toronto: Between the Lines Press.

Marcus, George E. 1995. "Ethnography in/of the World System: The Emergence of Multi-Sited Ethnography." *Annual Review of Anthropology* 24: 95–117.

Marule, Marie Smallface. 1984. "Traditional Indian Government." In *Pathways to Self-Determination*, edited by Leroy Little Bear, Menno Boldt, J. Anthony Long, 36–46. Toronto: University of Toronto Press.

Marx, Karl. 1977 [1897]. *Capital*, Vol. 1. Translated by Ben Fowkes. New York: Vintage Books.

———. 1975. "Concerning Feuerbach [Theses on Feuerbach]." In *Early Writings*. Edited by Quintin Hoare. New York: Vintage Books.

———. 1974. "The Eighteenth Brumaire of Louis Bonaparte." Translated by Ben Fowkes in *Surveys From Exile*. Edited by David Fernbach. New York: Vintage Books.

———. 1973 [1939]. *Grundrisse*. Translated by Martin Nicolaus. New York: Vintage Books.

McLeod, Neal. 2007. *Cree Narrative Memory*. Saskatoon: Purich Publishing.

Medicine, Beatrice. 2001. *Learning to Be an Anthropologist and Remaining "Native."* Urbana: University of Illinois Press.

Mills, Antonia. 1994. *Eagle Down Is Our Law*. Vancouver: University of British Columbia Press.

Monture-Angus, Patricia. 1995. *Thunder in My Soul*. Halifax: Fernwood.

Morris, Alexander. 1991. *The Treaties with the Indians of Canada*. Saskatoon: Fifth House Publishers.

Nadasday, Paul. 2003. *Hunters and Bureaucrats*. Vancouver: University of British Columbia Press.

Nancy, Jean-Luc. 1991. *The Inoperative Community*. Translated by Peter Connor et al. Minneapolis: University of Minnesota Press.

Passaro, Joanne. 1997. "'You can't take the subway to the field!': 'Village' epistemologies in the Global Village" in *Anthropological Locations: Boundaries and Grounds of a Field Science*. Edited by Akhil Gupta and James Ferguson, 147–62. Berkeley: University of California Press.

Rancière, Jacques. *Disagreement: Politics and Philosophy.* 1999. Minneapolis: University of Minnesota Press.

Ridington, Robin. 1990. *Little Bit Know Something.* Vancouver: Douglas and McIntyre.

Rushforth, Scott, and James S. Chisholm. 1991. *Cultural Persistence.* Tucson: University of Arizona Press.

Ryan, Joan. *Doing Things the Right Way.* 1995. Calgary: University of Calgary Press.

Sahlins, Marshall. 1972. *Stone Age Economics.* Chicago: Aldine-Atherton.

———. 1976. *Culture and Practical Reason.* Chicago: University of Chicago Press.

Said, Edward. 1979. *Orientalism.* New York: Vintage Books.

Sartre, Jean-Paul. 1978. *Critique of Dialectical Reason,* Vol. 1. Translated by Alan Sheridan-Smith. London: New Left Books.

Scott, James. 1985. *Weapons of the Weak.* New Haven, CT: Yale University Press.

Sharp, Henry. 2001. *Loon: Memory, Meaning and Reality in a Northern Dene Community.* Lincoln: University of Nebraska Press.

Silverman, Kaja. 1996. *The Threshold of the Visible World.* New York: Routledge.

Simpson, Audra. 2014. *Mohawk Interruptus.* Durham, NC: Duke University Press.

Slattery, Brian. 1987. "Understanding Aboriginal Rights." *Canadian Bar Review* 66 (4): 727–83.

Smith, Gavin. 1999. "Politically Engaged Social Enquiry and Images of Society." In *Confronting the Present: Towards a Politically Engaged Anthropology,* edited by Gavin Smith, 19–50. Oxford and New York: Berg.

Smith, Linda Tuhiwai. 1999. *Decolonizing Methodology*. London: Zed Books.

Spivak, Gayatri Chakravorty. 1999. *A Critique of Postcolonial Reason*. Cambridge, MA: Harvard University Press.

Taussig, Michael. 1986. *The Devil and Commodity Fetishism in South America*. Chapel Hill: University of North Carolina Press.

———. 1987. *Shamanism, Colonialism, and the Wild Man*. Chicago: University of Chicago Press.

———. 1992. *The Nervous System*. New York: Routledge.

———. 1994. *Mimesis and Alterity*. New York: Routledge.

Taylor, Diana. 2003. *The Archive and the Repertoire*. Durham, NC: Duke University Press.

Thompson, E.P. 1993. *Customs in Common*. New York: The New Press.

Tully, James. 2005. "Exclusion and Assimilation: Two Forms of Domination in Relation to Freedom." In *Political Exclusion and Domination*, edited by Melissa S. Williams and Stephen Macedo. New York: New York University Press. 191–229.

Unamuno, Miguel de. *The Tragic Sense of Life in Men and Nations*. 1972. Translated by Anthony Kerrigan. Princeton: Princeton University Press.

Waldram, James. *As Long as the Rivers Run: Hydro Electric Development and Native Communities in Western Canada*. 1988. Winnipeg: University of Manitoba Press.

Watkins, Mel, ed. 1977. *Dene Nation: The Colony Within*. Toronto: University of Toronto Press.

Wenzel, George. 1991. *Animal Rights, Human Rights*. Toronto: University of Toronto Press.

Wolfe, Eric. R. 1982. *Europe and the People without History.* Berkeley: University of California Press.

Young, Robert. 2001. *Postcolonialism.* Oxford: Blackwell Publishing.

CONTEMPORARY STUDIES ON THE NORTH
ISSN 1928-1722

CHRIS TROTT, SERIES EDITOR

5 *Report of an Inquiry into an Injustice: Begade Shutagot'ine and the Sahtu Treaty*, by Peter Kulchyski

4 *Sanaaq: An Inuit Novel*, by Mitiarjuk Nappaaluk

3 *Stories in a New Skin: Approaches to Inuit Literature*, by Keavy Martin

2 *Settlement, Subsistence, and Change among the Labrador Inuit: The Nunatsiavummiut Experience*, edited by David C. Natcher, Lawrence Felt, and Andrea Procter

1 *Like the Sound of a Drum: Aboriginal Cultural Politics in Denendeh and Nunavut*, by Peter Kulchyski